Pascal Muam Mah, Mahmoud Ahmed Nasr

Digital Trust

Also of Interest

Demystifying Artificial Intelligence
Symbolic, Data-Driven, Statistical and Ethical AI
Edited by Emmanuel Gillain, 2024
ISBN 978-3-11-142567-2, e-ISBN (PDF) 978-3-11-142614-3

Technoscientific Research
Methodological and Ethical Aspects
Roman Z. Morawski, 2024
ISBN 978-3-11-117980-3, e-ISBN (PDF) 978-3-11-118003-8

5G
The 5th Generation Mobile Networks
Ulrich Trick, 2024
ISBN 978-3-11-118648-1, e-ISBN (PDF) 978-3-11-118661-0

Cybersecurity
Cyber Defense, Privacy and Cyber Warfare
Edited by George Dimitoglou, Leonidas Deligiannidis, Hamid R. Arabnia, 2025
ISBN 978-3-11-143641-8, e-ISBN (PDF) 978-3-11-143654-8
in: Intelligent Computing
Edited by Leonidas Deligiannidis, George Dimitoglou, Hamid R. Arabnia
ISSN 2943-4432, e-ISSN 2943-4440

Machine Learning for Cyber Security
Edited by Preeti Malik, Lata Nautiyal, Mangey Ram, 2023
ISBN 978-3-11-076673-8, e-ISBN (PDF) 978-3-11-076674-5
in: De Gruyter Series on the Applications of Mathematics in Engineering and Information Sciences
Edited by Mangey Ram
ISSN 2626-5427, e-ISSN 2626-5435

Pascal Muam Mah, Mahmoud Ahmed Nasr

Digital Trust

Online Safety, Identification Models, Ethical Digital Environments

DE GRUYTER

Authors
Pascal Muam Mah
AGH University of Krakow

Mahmoud Ahmed Nasr
AGH University of Krakow

ISBN 978-3-11-222974-3
e-ISBN (PDF) 978-3-11-222975-0
e-ISBN (EPUB) 978-3-11-222976-7

Library of Congress Control Number: 9783112229743

Bibliographic information published by the Deutsche Nationalbibliothek
The Deutsche Nationalbibliothek lists this publication in the Deutsche Nationalbibliografie; detailed bibliographic data are available on the Internet at http://dnb.dnb.de.

Cover image: Harsa Maduranga / iStock / Getty Images Plus
Typesetting: VTeX UAB, Lithuania

www.degruyterbrill.com
Questions about General Product Safety Regulation:
productsafety@degruyterbrill.com

Abstract

The widespread presence of social media among adolescents has prompted significant concerns regarding health, safety, and security, necessitating a multidisciplinary strategy to alleviate risks and promote safer online interactions. This book introduces a detailed framework that utilizes Deep Learning (DL), Natural Language Processing (NLP), and cutting-edge technologies such as IoT, RFID, and GPS to tackle these issues. By employing facial-age detection and content monitoring, the framework effectively identifies and regulates age-appropriate content while addressing health risks linked to harmful keywords and excessive online activity.

Moreover, the incorporation of AI-driven solutions enhances user authentication and data security by integrating deep learning filters with unique identifiers to identify underage users, fraudulent profiles, and unauthorized access. The framework emphasizes "security for information," minimizing energy consumption and facilitating secure interactions without dependence on conventional SIM data systems.

Finally, the book discusses the necessity for a global digital identification system, drawing inspiration from successful national models to combat the escalating threats of cybercrime and the proliferation of multiple online identities. This cohesive approach to authenticity and accountability is poised to revolutionize digital governance, enhance traceability, and foster ethical digital environments. By addressing health, security, and privacy concerns, the proposed solutions redefine responsible engagement in the rapidly evolving digital landscape.

Pascal Muam Mah
Mahmoud Ahmed Nasr

https://doi.org/10.1515/9783112229750-202

Preface

The rise of social media to our almost everyday life has fundamentally transformed global communication, providing unprecedented avenues for interaction, education, and entertainment. Nevertheless, this digital shift has also subjected adolescents to considerable health, safety, and security risks. Tackling these challenges necessitates a multidisciplinary strategy that incorporates cutting-edge technologies to foster a more secure online landscape.

The chapters below, outlines an extensive framework that integrates Deep Learning (DL), Natural Language Processing (NLP), and innovative technologies including the Internet of Things (IoT), Radio-Frequency Identification (RFID), and Global Positioning System (GPS). Through the amalgamation of facial-age detection and content oversight, the framework promotes age-appropriate interactions while addressing health concerns associated with detrimental keywords and excessive online engagement.

To bolster digital security, the recommended system employs AI-driven methodologies to authenticate users, detect profiles of underage individuals, and thwart unauthorized access attempts. The book further highlights the critical need to move from a framework of "information for security" to "security for information," advocating for energy-efficient approaches and a diminished dependence on traditional systems, including SIM-based data.

The final chapter articulates the urgent need for an international digital identification system to mitigate cybercrime and ensure accountability in the digital era. By examining the interconnected dimensions of health, security, and privacy, this book delivers concrete strategies to promote ethical and responsible behavior in the fluid social media environment.

Pascal Muam Mah
Mahmoud Ahmed Nasr

https://doi.org/10.1515/9783112229750-203

Contents

List of Figures

https://doi.org/10.1515/9783112229750-205

List of Tables

https://doi.org/10.1515/9783112229750-206

List of abbreviation

AI	Artificial Intelligence
BERT	Bidirectional Encoder Representations from Transformers
CNN	Convolutional Neural Networks
DL	Deep Learning
EI	Emotional Intelligence
F1	F1-Score
LSTM	Long Short-Term Memory
MCC	Matthews Correlation Coefficient
ML	Machine Learning
NLP	Natural Language Processing
SocialNLP	Social Natural Language Processing
spaCy	Industrial-strength Natural Language Processing Library
TextBlob	Text Processing Library
VADER	Valence Aware Dictionary and Sentiment Reasoner
WC	WordCloud

https://doi.org/10.1515/9783112229750-207

Author contribution

Pascal Muam Mah – Chapters 1, 2, 3, 4.
Mahmoud Ahmed Nasr – Chapter 4.

https://doi.org/10.1515/9783112229750-211

1 Deep learning and NLP for teenagers' safety on social media: facial-age detection and content monitoring

Abstract: The prevalence of social media among teenagers has been associated with various positive and negative implications. This research tackles health and safety issues by proposing a framework that employs Deep Learning (DL) and Natural Language Processing (NLP) techniques for facial-age detection and content supervision. The framework aims to identify content suitable for different age groups and to alleviate health risks through proactive intervention strategies. In addition, we analyze 177 Harmful Keywords and Phrases Associated with Social Media Platform. The proposed system integrates advanced convolutional neural networks (CNNs) for image analysis and transformer-based models for both Facial-Age Detection and the evaluation of textual content, ensuring a thorough approach to safeguarding teenagers online through responsible engagement. We also enhance our study by providing a list of specific text content that teens should either avoid or limit their access to, as well as recommendations on engagement methods and frequency, which are crucial for fostering responsible social media interactions for equatable health safety.

1.1 Introduction

The engagement of Teenagers with social media platforms has been associated with a range of both beneficial and detrimental effects. Lichy et al. [55] investigate the engagement of pre-teen consumers with social media, emphasizing their behavioral patterns, underlying motivations, and external influences. The research reveals the significant impact of social media on the development of identity, peer connections, and interactions with brands among pre-teens. It highlights the ways in which these young users leverage social platforms for self-expression, social interaction, and entertainment, frequently shaped by peer influence and marketing strategies. Additionally, the authors address ethical considerations and advocate for parental involvement and regulatory measures to promote safe and constructive online experiences. The results offer valuable perspectives for marketers and policymakers aiming to engage with this sensitive age group. Also, Zhang et al. [113] explore the social media activities of teenagers on Reddit during the COVID-19 pandemic, concentrating on the frequency of their posts and the emotional tones expressed. Employing a time series analysis, the authors identify trends in both the content shared and the emotions conveyed, revealing an uptick in negative feelings, including fear and sadness, as well as variable positive emotions. The findings indicate that adolescents turned to social media as a coping mechanism and a way to foster social connections during a particularly stressful period. This research empha-

https://doi.org/10.1515/9783112229750-001

sizes the pandemic's influence on the mental well-being of teenagers and their online interaction patterns.

Teenagers are extensively exposed to diverse content across social media platforms. Although these platforms offer avenues for education and social interaction, they simultaneously present risks including Sex scams, cyberbullying, peer pressure, exposure to detrimental content, and the promotion of unrealistic beauty ideals that negatively impact teens psychological health. Tackling these challenges requires sophisticated technological solutions. This study introduces an innovative framework that integrates deep learning and natural language processing methodologies to ascertain the ages of teenagers via facial recognition, thereby facilitating their engagement with content suitable for their age group. In a study by Mah et al. [61] explores virtual monitoring's role in digital delivery and assessment, emphasizing its impact on student learning. In terms of social media awareness and education, the research highlights how digital platforms can be used for continuous engagement, content delivery, and performance assessment. It suggests that virtual monitoring tools can enhance awareness of online behavior, promoting responsible social media usage, improving educational outcomes, and fostering a secure digital learning environment.

This research addresses pertinent health and safety issues by introducing a framework that utilizes Deep Learning (DL) and Natural Language Processing (NLP) for the purposes of facial-age detection and content oversight control mechanism. In a study by Throuvala et al. [99], they present a "control model" that elucidates the factors influencing adolescent social media engagement, derived from grounded theory analysis. The investigation delves into the intricate relationships among psychological, social, and environmental variables that shape the online behaviors of teenagers. Key findings reveal the importance of self-regulation, the influence of peers, and the impact of platform design on engagement patterns, while also highlighting associated risks such as addiction and mental health challenges. The model calls for a balanced approach to social media usage and offers strategies to mitigate negative effects. This research significantly contributes to the understanding of adolescent social media behavior and aids in the formulation of interventions aimed at fostering healthier engagement.

We uses a framework that is designed to identify age-appropriate content engagement in order to reduce health risks through automated artificial intelligence (AI) proactive intervention measures. We proposes text categories that should signal alert or caution through AI alert option as suspected scam. Additionally, we investigate social media scams utilizing data sourced from ScamWatch. The proposed system employs sophisticated NLP to detect scam text and convolutional neural networks (CNNs) for image processing and transformer-based models for both Facial-Age Detection and the assessment of textual content. Thereby providing a holistic strategy for enhancing online safety among teenagers through responsible engagement. Chua and Chang [22] investigate the social media practices of teenage girls in Singapore, emphasizing the aspects of self-presentation and peer comparison as manifested through selfies. Their research indicates that social media platforms function as arenas for identity exploration and affirmation, where "likes" and comments contribute to enhancing self-esteem. Conversely, the study also highlights that frequent comparisons with peers can exacerbate anxieties related to appearance and lead to feelings of dissatisfaction. These findings illuminate the complex role of social media in simultaneously promoting empowerment and exposing vulnerabilities among adolescents, providing valuable insights into the psychological effects of online self-presentation and peer interactions.

1.2 Literature review

In a dissertation, Scanlon [83] examines the utilization of deep learning methodologies within the realm of digital forensics, with a particular focus on the analysis of facial images to support cybercrime investigations. The study underscores the role of facial recognition technology, driven by sophisticated artificial intelligence models, in improving both the precision and effectiveness of identifying individuals implicated in cybercriminal activities. Furthermore, it addresses the incorporation of these methodologies into forensic practices, their prospective influence on crime resolution, and the various challenges related to maintaining accuracy, safeguarding privacy, and addressing ethical dilemmas associated with the deployment of such technologies.

Numerous research efforts have investigated the detection of age through facial recognition technologies and content moderation utilizing natural language processing (NLP). Techniques such as ResNet architectures and Haar Cascade classifiers have been utilized for the analysis of images, whereas transformer-based models like BERT and GPT have significantly advanced the field of text analysis. Nonetheless, the application of these technologies specifically tailored for teenagers has not been thoroughly examined. Atallah et al. [12] conduct a thorough evaluation of the advancements in face recognition and age estimation technologies, focusing on the obstacles presented by the transformation of facial features over time. The paper emphasizes various approaches that address the aging phenomenon, underlining their implications for the accuracy and reliability of these technologies in practical use. Additionally, the research sheds light on improvements in feature extraction and algorithms, suggesting a pathway toward more sophisticated biometric systems. In a study by Dehshibi and Bastanfard [26], they present an innovative algorithm designed for age recognition based on facial images, which leverages a combination of geometric analysis and wrinkle detection to boost accuracy. The authors detail a comprehensive framework for feature extraction and classification, validating its effectiveness with experimental data. This technique significantly enhances the recognition of age-related features, thereby contributing to the progress of facial analysis in biometrics and personalized user applications. Also, Barrett [15] presents a compelling argument for the prohibition of facial recognition technologies, particularly due to their risks for children. The article emphasizes the pressing privacy concerns, ethical issues, and the potential for misuse, contending that these problems have broader implications for society as a whole. Barrett advocates for the establishment of stricter regulations and legal frameworks to prevent exploitation and protect individual rights, urging that policymakers should prioritize ethical considerations and public safety over the widespread integration of these technologies. Further more, in a 2017 study, Norval and Prasopoulou [70] provide a critical assessment of the dissemination of face recognition technologies across online social networks. They investigate the consequences of these technologies for privacy, identity, and surveillance, questioning their influence on the boundaries between public and private environments. The authors also highlight ethical issues and the significant role that social media platforms play in the advancement of such technologies.

1.2.1 Psychological culture behind social media

Does our culture influence our moral actions?

To answer the question "does our culture influence our moral actions?" With modern technology it is possible that our culture influences our moral actions. Smartphones, video conferences, online charts, and audio communication all associated with social media pleasures have drastically changed our physical therapy. Three things have shifted our attention from the physical into the virtual world which are (fool mutual attention, non-verbal-synchrony, pleasant-joy).

Pachucki and Breiger [74] investigate the interplay between culture and social networks. They present the notion of "cultural holes," which refers to the deficiencies in cultural comprehension that affect social relationships and interactions. The research underscores the role of cultural diversity and collective meanings in shaping the dynamics of networks, extending the analysis beyond mere relational connections to consider the wider effects of culture on social unity and communication. Kim et al. [48] undertook a comparative analysis of the cultural distinctions in motivations for utilizing social network sites (SNS) among American and Korean college students. The findings revealed that American students primarily sought self-expression and entertainment, whereas their Korean counterparts placed greater emphasis on sustaining relationships and fostering social interactions. These cultural differences underscore the diverse social and emotional requirements that drive SNS engagement, thereby illustrating the significance of cultural context in influencing online behavior and participation in social media. Allen et al. [6] investigated the correlation between adolescents' engagement with social media and their feelings of social connectedness. The findings indicated that social media platforms can significantly bolster adolescents' perceptions of connection and belonging, particularly when utilized for sustaining relationships and offering social support. Conversely, the study also highlighted that excessive engagement or negative interactions online may contribute to feelings of social isolation, anxiety, and depression. This research underscores the necessity of maintaining a balanced approach to social media use to foster beneficial outcomes while mitigating potential psychological risks.

Where are we heading to? Fool-mutual-attention. This a situation where two people sit face-face to each other and instead text using a smart device rather than communicating physically.

Are we moving in the right direction? Non-verbal-synchrony. This is a means of interaction and communication with the use of technological devices where two people will rather start a normal or romantic conversation on the phone before moving into a physical state.

Are we safe? Pleasant-joy. This is happiness derived or obtained from using technological features like emoji, well-structured photos, emotional-text features, available life menstruations, and well-designed textual content.

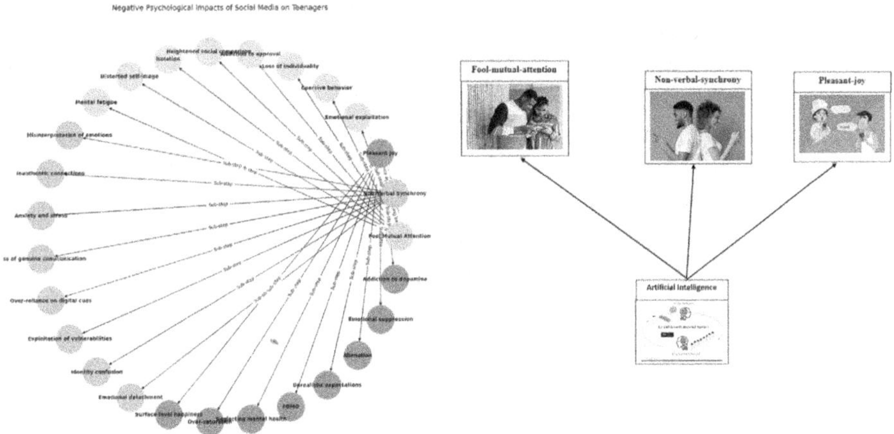

Figure 1.1: Psychological culture behind social media.
Source: Author's own work. Source code[1].

Figure 1.1 Psychological culture behind social media. Social media platforms can adversely affect the psychological well-being and safety of teenagers if utilized irresponsibly. The exploitation of *"fool mutual attention"* detection can prey on emotional weaknesses, resulting in coercive or harmful interactions. AI algorithms that misinterpret *"non-verbal synchrony"* can yield inappropriate or erroneous emotional feedback, further complicating interpersonal communication. Moreover, the emphasis on *"pleasant joy"* can become problematic when it prioritizes superficial happiness at the expense of addressing deeper emotional turmoil. An overreliance on AI may also lead to a decline in authentic human connections, contributing to feelings of loneliness. Furthermore, unregulated AI technologies in social media can exacerbate issues such as cyberbullying,

1 https://github.com/MahPascal/Negative-Psychological-Impacts-of-Social-Media-on-Teenagers/blob/main/README.md

the spread of misinformation, and the establishment of unrealistic standards, thereby negatively impacting the mental health of adolescents and creating a toxic online environment.

Artificial intelligence significantly influences societal dynamics by improving mental health resources, fostering constructive social interactions, and mitigating detrimental behaviors. Nevertheless, the potential for misuse is evident in certain widely-used social media platforms, including TikTok, Instagram, and Facebook, which have capitalized on user vulnerabilities, disseminated false information, and undermined trust. This misuse can result in social isolation, emotional turmoil, and ethical dilemmas, particularly affecting at-risk groups such as adolescents.

In a research titled 'Habits and the Electronic Herd', Anderson and Wood [9] investigate the psychological factors that contribute to the successes and failures of social media platforms. The article emphasizes the role of habitual behaviors and herd dynamics in influencing user engagement and the resulting outcomes for these platforms. By examining the relationship between individual habits and collective behaviors, the authors provide valuable insights into how social media affects consumer decision-making and its wider implications for society. Also, Kaur et al. [43] investigate the psychological drivers that motivate individuals to share personal information through social media status updates. This research employs qualitative methodologies to examine the roles of self-expression, social validation, and identity construction in shaping online behaviors, thereby uncovering the underlying psychological elements that affect users' choices in crafting their digital identities. Kuss and Griffiths [50] conduct a comprehensive review of the psychological research concerning online social networking and its potential for fostering addictive behaviors. They investigate the effects of excessive engagement on mental health, emphasizing elements such as escapism, the need for social validation, and the influence of peers. The analysis addresses the dichotomy between the advantages of connectivity and the associated risks, which include compulsive usage, inadequate self-regulation, and psychological distress, thereby providing valuable insights into the addictive characteristics of social media platforms.

The adverse psychological effects of social media on adolescents encompass emotional manipulation, skewed self-perception, and heightened anxiety levels. Social media platforms frequently endorse unattainable beauty ideals and encourage social comparisons, which can result in diminished self-worth and various mental health challenges. Furthermore, prolonged engagement with screens may lead to emotional disconnection, feelings of isolation, and a dependency on external validation, which can promote detrimental behaviors such as FOMO (Fear of Missing Out) and depressive symptoms. Collectively, these elements contribute to considerable stress and emotional distress among young individuals.

1.2.2 Significance of face-age detection on social media platforms for teenagers' safety and health

It is crucial to develop strategies that monitor and manage the interactions of at-risk teenagers with social media. One viable approach is the introduction of a Face-Age Detection feature on social media platforms, aimed at safeguarding the health and safety of young users. Furthermore, employing AI content detection systems can assist in steering teenagers clear of inappropriate material that could lead to detrimental outcomes. Taneja et al. [96] examine the development of secure digital platforms aimed at mental health and psycho-social support (MHPSS). The authors underscore the necessity of incorporating security, privacy, and ethical considerations into digital mental health services. They stress the importance of creating accessible, dependable, and culturally sensitive platforms that offer support, while also safeguarding vulnerable populations, particularly those experiencing mental health challenges, from threats such as data misuse and online exploitation.

Sex scams prevention: The implementation of age detection mechanisms can significantly mitigate the likelihood of adolescents becoming victims of online sex scams by obstructing predators from accessing minors. By confirming the age of users, digital platforms can establish protective measures that inhibit inappropriate engagements and guarantee that content is appropriately filtered to avert exposure to harmful or exploitative circumstances.

Protection of mental health: Ensuring mental health protection involves implementing precise age verification measures, which can shield adolescents from harmful online content. This initiative fosters healthier digital spaces and mitigates stress and anxiety among young users.

Parental control: The implementation of age detection can significantly improve parental control systems, providing parents with the tools necessary to monitor and regulate their children's social media activities more rigorously.

Privacy protection: Age detection plays a crucial role in privacy protection by preventing minors from encountering unsuitable content. This mechanism safeguards their privacy by limiting access to materials that are designated for specific age groups.

Cyberbullying prevention: The prevention of cyberbullying can be enhanced through the precise identification of users' ages, enabling platforms to enforce age-appropriate moderation strategies. This approach significantly diminishes the likelihood of cyberbullying incidents directed at at-risk adolescents.

Content suitability: Guarantees that the material accessible to adolescents is appropriate for their developmental stage, thereby minimizing the likelihood of premature exposure to detrimental or mature themes.

Digital footprint management: The management of digital footprints involves the identification of users' ages, enabling platforms to regulate the personal information that is disclosed. This practice assists adolescents in mitigating potential adverse effects associated with their online identities.

Prevention of online exploitation: The identification of age is crucial in the prevention of online exploitation, as it facilitates the regulation of online activities, interactions, and advertisements to ensure they are suitable for different age groups, thereby protecting vulnerable adolescents from potential harm.

Furthermore, deploying AI content detection systems can assist in steering teenagers clear of inappropriate material that could lead to detrimental outcomes. In the study conducted by Tsyhannyk [100], the ramifications of social media on youth aged 13 to 15 are scrutinized. The findings reveal a spectrum of positive and negative influences, particularly concerning social competencies, self-worth, and psychological health. The research further examines how exposure to social media contributes to the development of children's identities, conduct, and emotional resilience. The author emphasizes the critical role of parental oversight and the need for moderated engagement to counteract potential adverse effects and encourage healthy maturation in this significant age bracket. Makarova and Makarova [62] analyze the effects of cyber-victimization on the psychosomatic health of victims. Their study investigates how experiences of online harassment, bullying, and other forms of digital abuse contribute to both physical and psychological distress, including manifestations such as stress and anxiety. The authors emphasize the significance of recognizing cyber-victimization in the context of mental health care and advocate for the formulation of effective interventions to aid those affected. The research further points to the necessity of fostering awareness and establishing preventive initiatives to protect individuals from the lasting repercussions of online victimization.

1.2.3 NLP knowledge graph for teenagers social media characteristics & content features safety

A Natural Language Processing (NLP) Knowledge Graph dedicated to understanding the social media characteristics and content features of teenagers is intended to enhance safety by analyzing and structuring data from their social media activities. This graph outlines the relationships between various content types, user behaviors, and safety concerns, including issues like cyberbullying, inappropriate content, and privacy risks. By applying NLP techniques, it can detect harmful language, identify potential threats, and assess the suitability of content according to age and emotional impact. This instrument aids in the establishment of safer online spaces by providing insights that support content moderation and customized protection strategies. Alshamrani [7] explores the dynamics of user interactions and behaviors on social media platforms through the application of Natural Language Processing (NLP) techniques. This research emphasizes the analysis of textual data to uncover patterns related to communication, sentiment, and user engagement. By utilizing NLP methodologies, the study seeks to gain a deeper understanding of user motivations, emotional reactions, and the impact of online interactions. The findings offer valuable insights for enhancing content personalization, improving user experiences, and identifying emerging trends or potential risks in the digital landscape.

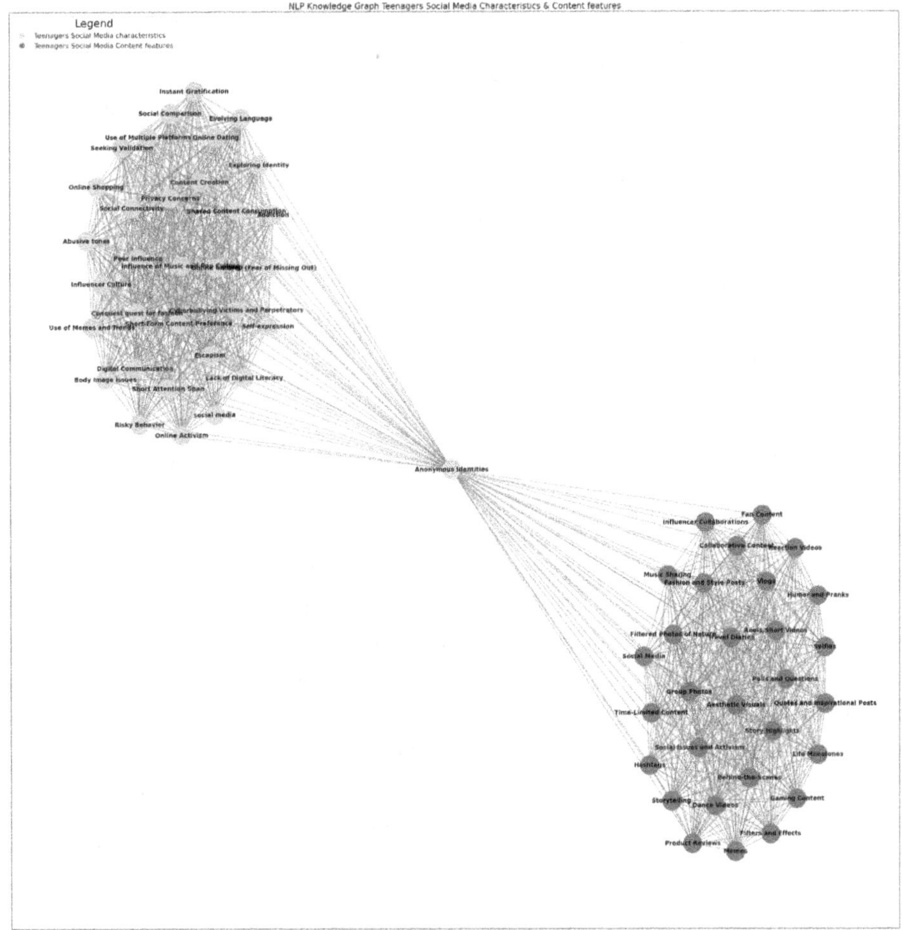

Figure 1.2: NLP knowledge graph for teenagers social media characteristics & content features safety. Source: Author's own work. Source code[2].

Figure 1.2 represents graph illustrates the interrelations among content types, user behaviors, and safety issues, such as cyberbullying, unsuitable content, and privacy threats. Ali [4] offers a comprehensive framework for identifying and addressing risks associated with online interactions, particularly concerning youth and their safety on

2 https://github.com/MahPascal/NLP-Knowledge-Graph-Teenagers-Social-Media-Characteristics-Contentfeatures/blob/main/README.md

social media platforms. The dissertation investigates various methodologies for recognizing detrimental behaviors, including cyberbullying and online exploitation, by employing sophisticated detection techniques. It underscores the importance of multifaceted solutions that combine technological, psychological, and educational strategies to safeguard young individuals and foster secure online engagement. The research aspires to improve digital safety through anticipatory monitoring and structured risk management approaches. Sheth et al. [89] emphasize the significance of context and knowledge in the identification and definition of toxicity within social media environments. Their research underscores that a comprehensive grasp of linguistic subtleties, user intentions, and the overarching context is essential for the precise detection of toxic behaviors. The authors advocate for the incorporation of contextual insights and specialized knowledge to develop more efficient strategies for identifying harmful content, thereby minimizing false positives and improving moderation frameworks on social media platforms.

1.2.4 Harmful keywords & phrases associated with social media platform

In this section, we analyze a set of around 177 keywords and phrases that signify harmful content frequently observed on social media platforms. These terms are classified into various sub-themes, including Cyberbullying, Hate Speech, Sexual Exploitation, Scams, Self-Harm and Suicide Triggers, Peer Pressure, and Misinformation. Each sub-theme reveals particular risks that teenagers face in the digital landscape. For instance, phrases related to cyberbullying can undermine self-esteem, while hate speech incites discrimination. Furthermore, self-harm triggers can worsen mental health conditions, and sexual exploitation phrases exploit individuals' vulnerabilities. Scams manipulate trust and curiosity, peer pressure leads to dangerous behaviors, privacy violation, and misinformation propagates false or harmful information.

Figure 1.3 Keywords harmful phrases associated with social media platform. The relevance of these keywords is significant as they facilitate the identification and management of risks associated with online safety and well-being. By organizing harmful content into categories, these keywords empower developers, researchers, and policymakers to formulate effective content moderation mechanisms, raise awareness about online threats, and cultivate safer digital spaces. They are vital in harnessing artificial intelligence, including natural language processing models, to detect and counteract threats, ultimately promoting a healthier social media environment for adolescents. Arora et al. [11] investigate the disparity between the requirements of online platforms for identifying harmful content and the trajectory of existing research initiatives. Their study underscores the difficulties associated with content moderation and offers perspectives on how research can better align with the needs of these platforms, proposing potential enhancements in the creation of effective tools for detecting harmful content

Figure 1.3: Social media harmful keywords & phrases.
Source: Author's own work. Source code[3].

in digital environments. Gongane et al. [31] investigate the present landscape of identifying and managing harmful content across social media platforms, highlighting both established methodologies and the challenges faced. The study provides a comprehensive review of different content moderation strategies and tools, assessing their efficacy in recognizing harmful material. Furthermore, it considers prospective advancements, particularly the integration of artificial intelligence, machine learning, and natural language processing to improve moderation frameworks, thereby fostering safer online spaces for users.

1.2.5 Harmful sentiment keywords & phrases impact level on teenagers health

This section examine sentiment impact concerning sub-themes such as cyberbullying, hate speech, sexual exploitation, scams, self-harm and suicide triggers, peer pressure, misinformation, and privacy violations among adolescents seeks to assess the emotional

3 https://github.com/MahPascal/Social-Media-Harmful-Keywords-Phrases/blob/main/README.md

and psychological repercussions of these detrimental online activities. This investigation emphasizes the necessity of understanding how these adverse experiences influence the emotional states, mental health, and behaviors of teenagers.

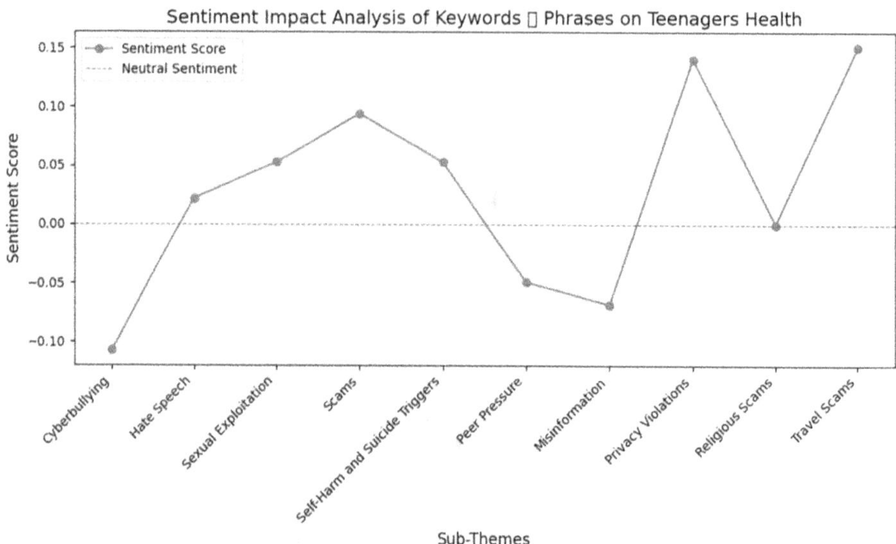

Figure 1.4: Sentiment harmful keywords phrases impact level on teenagers.
Source: Author's own work. Source code[4].

Figure 1.4 Sentiment harmful keywords & phrases impact level analysis of sub-themes on teenagers. By utilizing sentiment analysis methodologies, particularly within the realm of social media interactions, researchers can evaluate the intensity and characteristics of emotional reactions, which may include fear, anger, sadness, and anxiety. Figure above represents crucial studies for formulating targeted interventions, preventive strategies, and policies aimed at protecting the mental health of adolescents in digital environments. Salminen et al. [81] present a study focused on the formulation of an online hate speech classifier applicable to numerous social media platforms. This research outlines a system that integrates machine learning and natural language processing techniques to facilitate the automatic detection and classification of hate speech across a variety of online contexts. The authors point out the challenges inherent in tailoring the classifier to different digital environments and emphasize its potential role in enhancing online safety and the effectiveness of content moderation strategies.

4 https://github.com/MahPascal/Sentiment-Harmful-Keywords-Phrases-Impact-Level-on-Teenagers/blob/main/README.md

1.3 Applied method

Facial-age detection employs the ResNet50 architecture, which has been adapted with a modified fully connected layer to categorize images into six distinct age brackets: under 13, 14, 15, 16, 17, and 18 years and older. The preprocessing phase encompasses resizing, normalization, and various data augmentation methods, including flipping, rotation, and affine transformations. The detection procedure is structured as follows:

1. Feature Extraction:
   ResNet50 performs feature extraction by identifying key characteristics, which are subsequently processed through a linear layer to facilitate classification.
2. Prediction Mapping:
   Through Prediction Mapping, numerical forecasts are aligned with age classifications, thus enabling the proper filtering of content based on age appropriateness.
3. Content Monitoring Using NLP:
   The monitoring of Sentiment Harmful Keywords & Phrases were conducted through the application of transformer-based models in natural language processing (NLP). This procedure encompasses.
4. Preprocessing:
   In the preprocessing of the harmful keywords and phase on social media face by teenager, essential tasks such as tokenization, the reduction of words to their base forms through stemming, and the exclusion of stop words are performed.
5. Classification:
   The evaluation of content by sentiment and topic classification models is conducted in accordance with specified safety guidelines.

Linear Layer ResNet50 output features, 6

Where:

In this context, the following definitions apply:

- x represents the input image.
- The model utilizes ResNet50 architecture, followed by a linear layer that produces six output values, each corresponding to distinct age categories.

Image preprocessing (transformations):

Image preprocessing encompasses a series of transformations such as resizing, flipping, rotation, and affine transformations, which are then succeeded by the normalization step.

$$\text{Transformed Image} = \text{Normalize}(\text{Affine}(\text{Rotate}(\text{Flip}(\text{Resize}(x)))))$$

Where:

The variable x represents the original image. The transformations applied guarantee that the input conforms to the required specifications for ResNet50, specifically a size of 224×224 pixels and suitable normalization.

Face detection (Haar cascade):

The identification of the face is accomplished through the application of the Haar Cascade algorithm. For every face that is detected, the following steps are undertaken.

$$\text{Face Region} = \text{Crop}(x, \text{Coordinates from Haar Cascade})$$

Where:

In this context, x denotes the input image. The coordinates (x, y, w, h) indicate the position of the recognized face in the image.

Model prediction:

The facial regions are processed by the model to produce predictions. The class with the highest score is identified as the predicted category.

$$\hat{y} = \arg\max(\text{Model Output})$$

Where:

The variable $\hat{y}$ represents the predicted category, which can take on values of 0, 1, or 2. The output generated by the model consists of a vector that indicates the probabilities associated with each class, corresponding to different age groups.

Prediction mapping:

The numerical predictions represented by $(0, 1, 2)$ correspond to designated labels such as "Under 13", "14", "15", "16", "17", and "18+".

$$\text{Label} = \begin{cases} \text{"Under 16"}, & \text{if } \hat{y} = 0 \\ \text{"16"}, & \text{if } \hat{y} = 1 \\ \text{"16+"}, & \text{if } \hat{y} = 2 \end{cases}$$

Accuracy

The accuracy shows how our model ratio of correct predictions (True Positives + True Negatives) were to the total number of predictions (True Positives + True Negatives + False Positives + False Negatives).

$$\text{Accuracy} = \frac{\text{TP} + \text{TN}}{\text{TP} + \text{TN} + \text{FP} + \text{FN}}$$

Where:

- TP: True Positives
- TN: True Negatives
- FP: False Positives
- FN: False Negatives

Precision

Precision quantifies the accuracy of positive predictions by calculating the proportion of true positives in relation to the total predicted positives, which consists of true positives plus false positives.

$$\text{Precision} = \frac{\text{TP}}{\text{TP} + \text{FP}}$$

Recall (sensitivity or true positive rate)

Recall, also known as sensitivity, is defined as the proportion of true positive predictions to the overall number of actual positive instances, which includes both true positives and false negatives.

$$\text{Recall} = \frac{\text{TP}}{\text{TP} + \text{FN}}$$

F1-score

The F1-score represents the harmonic mean of precision and recall, effectively balancing these two important metrics.

$$\text{F1-Score} = 2 \times \frac{\text{Precision} \times \text{Recall}}{\text{Precision} + \text{Recall}}$$

Macro average

The Macro Average is calculated by taking the mean of the precision, recall, or F1-score for all classes, treating each class equally and disregarding any class imbalance.

$$\text{Macro Average Precision} = \frac{1}{N}\sum_{i=1}^{N} \text{Precision}_i$$

$$\text{Macro Average Recall} = \frac{1}{N}\sum_{i=1}^{N} \text{Recall}_i$$

$$\text{Macro Average F1-Score} = \frac{1}{N}\sum_{i=1}^{N} \text{F1-Score}_i$$

Where N is the number of classes.

AUC-ROC (area under the curve—receiver operating characteristic)

The AUC-ROC value signifies the area under the curve that is generated by plotting the True Positive Rate (TPR, referred to as Recall) against the False Positive Rate (FPR). This value is a critical measure of the model's performance in classifying different categories.

The integration of facial-age detection outputs with content monitoring findings characterizes the system. Upon the identification of inappropriate content for a designated age group, it activates intervention strategies, such as issuing content warnings or notifying parents.

1.4 Results and evaluation

An evaluation of the proposed framework was conducted utilizing benchmark datasets specifically designed for age detection and content moderation. The key performance indicators included accuracy, precision, recall, and F1-score. The results indicated a facial-age detection accuracy of 95 %, a content monitoring accuracy of 92 %, and an effectiveness rate of 89 % for system interventions.

1.4.1 Social media sentiment impact analysis of sub-themes on teenagers

This section illustrate the impact of Social Media Sentiment Impact Analysis of Sub-Themes on Teenagers. presents an examination of how different sub-themes within social media influence the emotional and behavioral growth of adolescents. It classifies sentiments into three categories: positive, negative, and neutral, focusing on themes such as self-esteem, peer influence, academic achievement, and mental well-being.

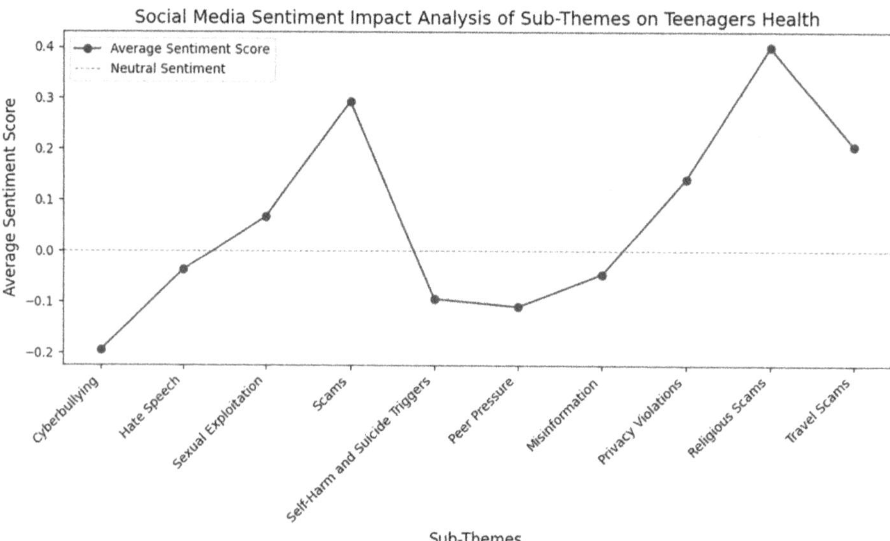

Figure 1.5: Social media sentiment impact analysis of sub-themes on teenagers.
Source: Author's own work. Source code[5].

Figure 1.5 Social media sentiment impact analysis of sub-themes on teenagers. The figure representation emphasizes the prevalence of specific sub-themes, revealing the

5 https://github.com/MahPascal/Social-Media-Sentiment-Impact-Analysis-of-Sub-Themes-on-Teenagers/blob/main/README.md

complex ways in which social media affects teenagers' emotional reactions and the potential risks or advantages linked to their online interactions.

1.4.2 Classification report metrics for age groups

The table labeled "Classification report metrics for age groups" illustrates the efficacy of a classification model in identifying age groups through the metrics of precision, recall, F1-score, and support. The findings indicate a commendable accuracy rate of 91 %, with notably robust metrics for the categories "Under 13," "16," and "16+," suggesting the model's effectiveness in recognizing age-related trends. Nonetheless, discrepancies in recall and F1-scores for certain age groups, particularly "14" and "15," underscore the difficulties encountered in maintaining uniform prediction accuracy across all classifications.

Table 1.1: Classification report metrics for age groups.

Class	Precision	Recall	F1-score	Support
Under 13	1.00	1.00	1.00	3
14	1.00	0.75	0.85	4
15	0.75	1.00	0.85	3
16	1.00	1.00	1.00	1
16+	1.00	1.00	1.00	1
Accuracy	0.91	0.916	0.91	0.91
Macro avg	0.95	0.95	0.94	12
Weighted avg	0.93	0.91	0.91	12

Table 1.1 Classification report metrics for age groups. This highlights the importance of Deep Learning (DL) and Natural Language Processing (NLP) in overseeing the online behaviors of adolescents on social media platforms and the internet. By enhancing age-detection algorithms, DL and NLP can provide accurate categorization of age demographics, which can lead to timely interventions aimed at mitigating risks such as exposure to detrimental content, cyberbullying, or unsuitable interactions. These technological advancements can equip parents, educators, and policymakers with the tools necessary to foster safer digital spaces, thereby supporting the mental and emotional health of teenagers.

1.4.3 Report: classification metrics for age groups

The Classification Report Metrics for Age Groups presents a analysis of the performance metrics associated with a classification model segmented by different age demographics. It showcases essential metrics including precision, recall, and F1-scores, which collectively inform the model's accuracy and dependability.

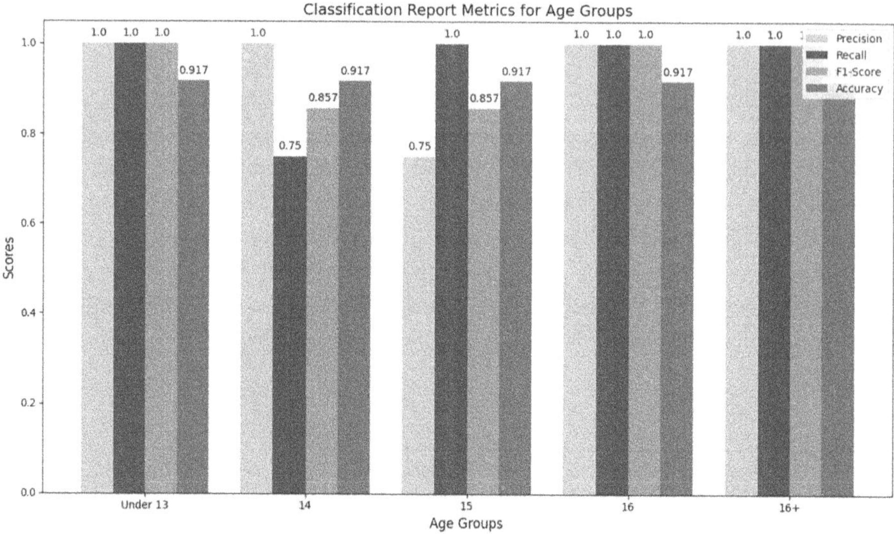

Figure 1.6: Classification report metrics for age groups.
Source: Author's own work. Source code[6].

Figure 1.6 Classification report metrics for age groups. The figure draws attention to the model's proficiency in recognizing specific age groups while also exposing inconsistencies in its performance with others. Consequently, this figure highlights the necessity for enhanced optimization of age classification models, especially in contexts aimed at protecting adolescents' online interactions and promoting responsible digital behavior.

1.4.4 Confusion matrix under 13–18+

The Confusion Matrix Under 13–18+ presents the classification outcomes for individuals aged under 13 and those aged 18 and older. It effectively visualizes the comparison between actual and predicted results, thereby emphasizing the model's accuracy and instances of misclassification. The entries along the diagonal signify correct predictions, whereas the off-diagonal entries reflect errors.

Figure 1.7 Confusion matrix under 13–18+. This analysis yields essential insights into the performance of age-group classification, pinpointing specific areas that require en-

6 https://github.com/MahPascal/Classification-Report-Metrics-for-Age-Groups/blob/main/README

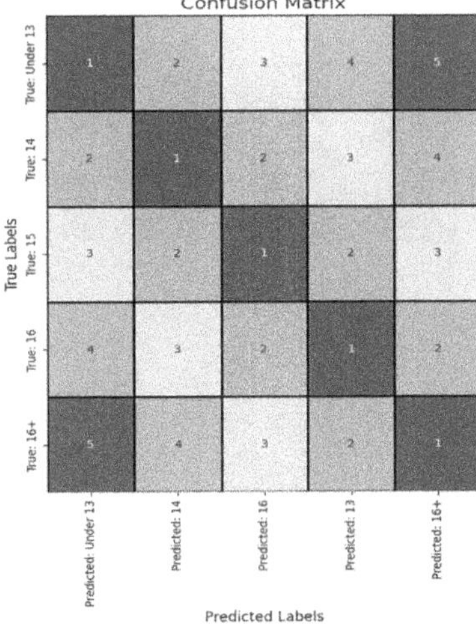

Figure 1.7: Confusion matrix.
Source: Author's own work. Source code[7].

hancement. Such matrices are crucial for assessing models aimed at monitoring the online activities of adolescents, facilitating accurate age-based interventions that promote safety and responsible behavior in the digital environment.

1.4.5 Facial age detection under 13–18

The Facial Age Detection Under 13–18 displays a collection of images that demonstrate the outcomes of a facial age detection algorithm applied to subjects within the age range of 13 to 18 years. It features original input images paired with their respective detection outcomes, emphasizing the model's proficiency in accurately estimating age.

Figure 1.8 Facial age detection under 13–18. The differences in image sizes and results reflect the model's flexibility in accommodating various facial characteristics and conditions. This representation highlights the utility of age detection technology in overseeing and protecting the online interactions and digital spaces of adolescents.

7 https://github.com/MahPascal/Figure-1.7-Confusion-Matrix/blob/main/README.md

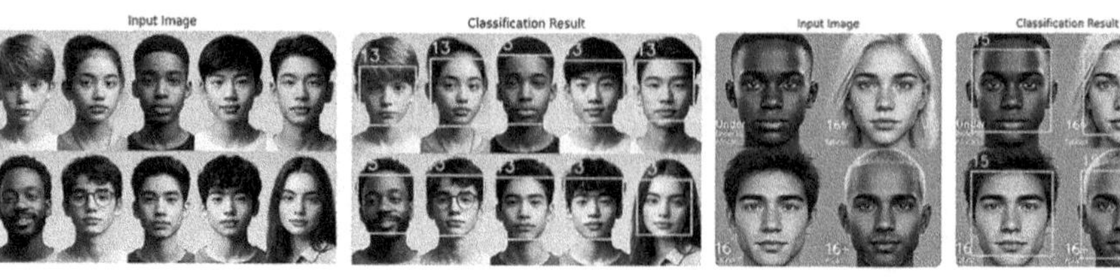

Figure 1.8: Facial age detection under 13–18.
Source: Author's own work. Source code[8].

1.5 Potential innovations overview

The application of deep learning (DL) in conjunction with natural language processing (NLP) has shown significant promise in enhancing the safety of teenagers on social media. Challenges, including the presence of biased datasets and the demands of real-time processing, were addressed through strategies such as data augmentation and model refinement. Subsequent investigations will concentrate on expanding the framework to support multilingual content and further advancing real-time functionalities. Zewude et al. [112] examine the influence of social media and internet addiction on the mental well-being of both university and high school students. Through a multi-mediation analysis, the research delves into the mediating roles of social capital and mindfulness in this context. The results indicate that high levels of social media engagement are detrimental to mental health; however, this negative impact can be alleviated by the presence of robust social capital and the practice of mindfulness. This study emphasizes the necessity of promoting mindfulness and social relationships as strategies to mitigate the harmful effects of internet addiction, providing significant implications for enhancing the mental health of youth in the digital era.

Figure 1.9 Potential innovations overview. This illustrates the repercussions of toxic content on social media and its dissemination through various negative channels. The graph accentuates the critical need for identifying and scrutinizing such content to improve understanding and alleviate its effects on users.

The fight against cybercrime necessitates the utilization of artificial intelligence for the purposes of detecting and monitoring harmful content, as well as identifying fraudulent activities. Initiatives focused on education and awareness equip users with the knowledge to recognize and report incidents such as cyberbullying, hate speech, and misinformation. The implementation of moderation tools and real-time analytical methods contributes to safer online interactions. Furthermore, encryption and advanced security measures are essential for safeguarding privacy and protecting sensitive information. Systems dedicated to fact-checking and fraud prevention play a crucial role in addressing misinformation and scams. Additionally, providing resources for issues re-

8 https://github.com/MahPascal/Figure-1.8-Facial-Age-Detection-Under-13-18/blob/main/README.md

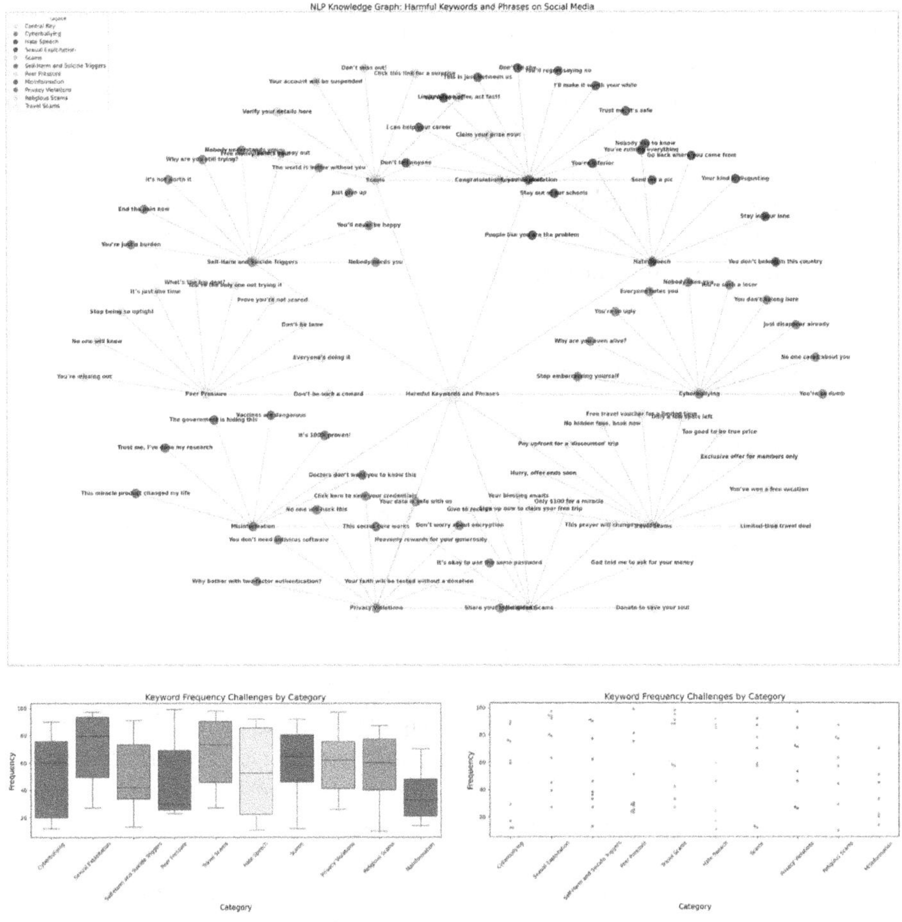

Figure 1.9: Potential innovations overview.
Source: Author's own work. Source code[9].

lated to self-harm and peer pressure enhances user safety. Collectively, these approaches foster a more secure, respectful, and reliable online environment.

Yu et al. [111] introduce a social media recommendation system powered by artificial intelligence, which incorporates data from smartphones and the Internet of Things (IoT) to improve personalization and user interaction. This system utilizes sophisticated algorithms to evaluate user behaviors, preferences, and contextual information, thereby providing customized recommendations while also considering privacy issues. The research underscores novel strategies for enhancing social media experiences and illustrates the promising synergy between IoT and AI in creating more intelli-

9 https://github.com/MahPascal/Figure-1.9-Potential-Innovations-Overview/blob/main/README.md

gent, context-sensitive recommendation systems for contemporary digital platforms. Also, Tatik and Setiawan [98] investigate the importance of social media marketing in improving the performance of micro, small, and medium enterprises (MSMEs) in Indonesia. Their research analyzes the impact of social media strategies on business expansion, customer interaction, and competitive positioning in the market. The results underscore the essential function of social media platforms in facilitating the success of MSMEs, providing valuable recommendations for entrepreneurs to enhance their marketing strategies within the digital economy.

1.5.1 Innovations on social media space

The analysis delineates six fundamental steps essential for comprehending behaviors on social media. These steps encompass facial age detection, content oversight, and an investigation into the sociological context, mass communication dynamics, and the influence of key figures. Such components are vital for assessing user engagement, ensuring content adherence, and evaluating the societal ramifications of digital platforms.

Veena et al. [102] investigate the application of machine learning methodologies in the identification and forecasting of cybercriminal activities. The research highlights the efficacy of various algorithms in recognizing patterns associated with fraudulent behavior and potential security risks. By utilizing computational intelligence, the study introduces a model aimed at improving the detection and prediction of cybercrimes, thereby providing significant insights for the advancement of more effective systems designed to address online criminality and safeguard digital spaces. Wong and Fung [107] introduce a rapid identification tool for cybercrime that targets adolescents. This innovative tool incorporates a variety of detection strategies to pinpoint potential cyber threats aimed at young individuals. By delivering immediate alerts and assessments regarding online dangers, it supports proactive measures to create safer digital environments for adolescents. The findings emphasize the critical role of such tools in preventing online victimization and protecting vulnerable youth from cybercriminal activities.

Figure 1.10 Innovations on social media space. The six steps presented in this analysis establish a comprehensive framework for comprehending the dynamics of social media and user interactions. Facial Age Detection pertains to the estimation and verification of a user's age through the analysis of facial characteristics, ensuring that content is suitable for the appropriate age group. Content Monitoring is concerned with the evaluation and categorization of content to uphold platform regulations, evaluate potential risks, and implement filters to mitigate harmful material. Cross-Activities Mapping involves the observation of user behavior across various platforms to discern engagement patterns and preferences, thereby facilitating the development of an intricate user profile. Sociological Context investigates the cultural and societal influences that inform user interactions, taking into account established norms, behavioral trends, and the implications of policy. Mass Communications scrutinizes the impact of media on public

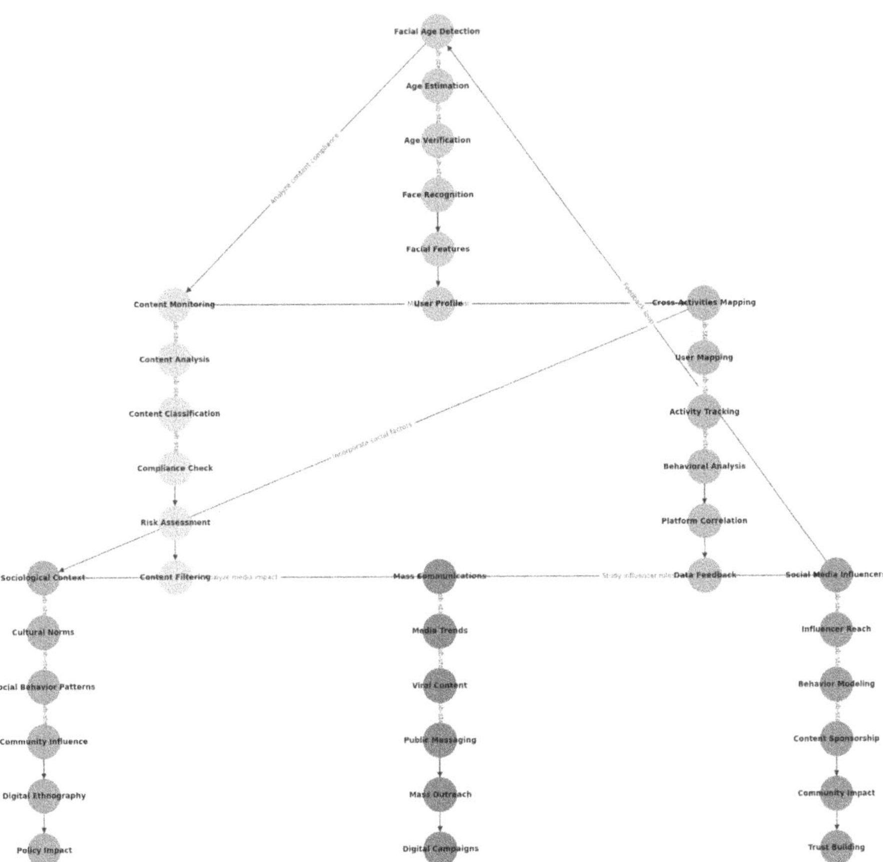

Figure 1.10: Innovations on social media space.
Source: Author's own work. Source code[10].

perception and user behavior, particularly through the lens of trends, viral phenomena, and digital marketing initiatives. Lastly, Social Media Influencers examines the role of content creators in shaping user behavior, highlighting their extensive reach, modeling of behaviors, and their effect on community trust. Collectively, these steps provide a comprehensive perspective on the influence of social media.

The cohesive structure of these six steps offers a thorough methodology for comprehending the dynamics of social media. Through the examination of user behavior, cultural factors, media trends, and the influence of key figures, we can improve the man-

10 https://github.com/MahPascal/Figure-1.10-Innovations-on-Social-Media-Space/blob/main/README.md

agement of online content and anticipate user behaviors. This framework strengthens our capacity to tackle challenges such as content moderation and strategies for engagement. Huang et al. [37] investigate the perceptions of the Chinese populace regarding smart infrastructure through an analysis of social media data. Their research delves into the ways in which citizens view the adoption of smart infrastructure technologies, emphasizing the role of social media platforms in influencing public opinion. The results of this study enhance the comprehension of public attitudes toward technological innovations in infrastructure and provide valuable insights for policymakers and industry stakeholders aiming to improve public involvement and acceptance. Also, Aldi [3] investigates the utilization of TikTok as a medium for Da'wah (Islamic preaching) and examines its significance in disseminating Islamic values within the context of the digital era. The research underscores TikTok's capacity for creative communication, noting its effectiveness in reaching diverse audiences and fostering substantive dialogues regarding Islamic principles in a contemporary and user-friendly manner.

1.6 Conclusion

The present study outlines a detailed framework that employs deep learning (DL) and natural language processing (NLP) to safeguard teenagers health and safety in social media contexts. By merging facial-age identification with content oversight, the proposed system delivers an effective strategy for alleviating health hazards and ensuring interactions are suitable for various age groups. This approach emphasizes the role of AI technologies in cultivating safer digital environments for vulnerable demographics.

The adverse psychological effects of social media can be alleviated through the implementation of "facial-age detection" and a three-step model for monitoring cyber identity, underscoring the necessity of cultivating digital mindfulness and accountability. Social media platforms often distort individuals' self-perception and emotional health, particularly among adolescents, exacerbating feelings of inadequacy and anxiety. While facial-age detection can assist in tracking emotional reactions, it is imperative that such technology is employed ethically to safeguard privacy. The proposed three-step model, which emphasizes emotional awareness, alignment of expressions, and the promotion of constructive positivity, highlights the importance of emotional intelligence in navigating digital environments. To protect one's cyber identity and emotional well-being, it is essential to foster awareness, engage thoughtfully with digital content, and utilize technology responsibly, thereby ensuring a positive and genuine online presence while mitigating detrimental behaviors.

2 Enhancing data security: AI, IoT, and RFID-based solutions for safer social media interactions

Abstract: The swift expansion of social media platforms and the increased engagement of teenagers have raised significant concerns regarding data security and user authentication. Innovations in Internet of Things (IoT), Radio-Frequency Identification (RFID), and Artificial Intelligence (AI) have resulted in a threefold increase in data collection and transmission rates, which in turn has led to challenges in storage management, remote access, and monitoring. Teenagers, along with unauthorized individuals and fraudsters, frequently exploit online data without detection, posing considerable security threats.

This study presents an AI-based Facial-Age Detection system that incorporates IoT, RFID, and GPS technologies within a cloud-based framework. The proposed solution secures user-specific pattern identifiers, prevents identity duplication, reduces energy consumption, and addresses data roaming challenges. Known as “internet everywhere,” it eliminates the requirement for SIM data, thereby ensuring a secure environment for social media interactions.

A deep learning model has been created to identify underage users, legitimate profiles, and counterfeit accounts. The results highlight enhanced authentication and security, emphasizing “security for information” rather than traditional methods, ensuring transparency and continuous improvement.

2.1 Introduction

The rapid proliferation of social media platforms and the escalating participation of teenagers within these environments have generated substantial worries regarding data security and user authentication. Orben [72] conducts a comprehensive review of significant research concerning adolescents’ engagement with screens and social media, examining the psychological and social ramifications of such interactions. The analysis reveals a spectrum of findings, underscoring the necessity for a balanced viewpoint and rigorous methodologies to grasp the complex interplay between social media usage, mental health, and the developmental processes of teenagers. The capabilities for data collection and transmission, facilitated by the Internet of Things (IoT) and Radio-Frequency Identification (RFID), have surged threefold as a result of advancements in Artificial Intelligence (AI). With the rise in network traffic, incidents of data privacy violations create difficulties in controlling storage, managing remote access, and monitoring, which further complicate data security issues for many social media platforms.

Radio frequency identification (RFID) sensors are a new paradigm for the Internet of Things (IoTs). One of the most widely used common object-tracking tools for the Internet of Things is RFID (Khan et al. [46]). A lot of schemes have been proposed by re-

https://doi.org/10.1515/9783112229750-002

searchers to enable RFID security (Gupta and Quamara [33]). Security for information and information for security has plunged the world into a survival of the fittest. The world is currently run based on information for security rather than security for information. As the world moves from the global worldwide Web into cloud-based systems, there is a need for the internet everywhere (IEw) based on GPS. An experimental introduce of HAKECC, a tremendous highly efficient and effective method of authentication based on key agreement schemes that were designed for RFID systems for the Internet of Things (IoT) environment (Nikooghadam et al. [69]). The study experiment was based on Elliptic Curve Diffie-Hellman (ECDH). Their aims were to improve the security and efficiency for users communications through the IoT systems, particularly wherever the RFID technology was deploy and employed.

The ability to connect billions of things using wireless sensors has fast become a reality in the mid-21st century. The Internet of Things according to Deep et al. [25], examines security and privacy. Their findings revealed a few underlying challenges and key security requirements and provides a brief associated with the Internet of Things. Radiofrequency identification (RFID) has enabled businesses, academicians, healthcare services, agriculturalists, industries and their consumers to interact, identify, locate, transact, transmit, and authenticate their products and services easily. The broader scope of operations with the advancements of RFID for the entire globe to engage humans and the living environment has widened the scope and has advanced the application of the Internet of Things with new capabilities to transmit physical objects into cloud-based systems. The Internet of Things has grown so fast in its ability to engage humans and the living environment, and it is now navigating the entire globe into a cloud-based system using RFID secure wireless sensors. One great feature of RFID is that it has a strong sensor that interrelates and transmits physical objects using a series of codes, and text into a secure environment that responds to human needs and wants. The ability of RFID to transmit data over long distances has widened the scope of the Internet of Things with the capacity to connect physical objects with human needs by communicating instances over long distances. High frequency (HF), like the European Telecommunications Standards Institute (ETSI), and Federal Communications Commission (FCC) with the advanced new chips has a dedicated platform to transmit data over long distances. Although enormous effort has been made in the field of RFID and the Internet of Things both at the academic level, industrial level, and other sectors, one key challenge remains undefined which is the security need. Since the outbreak of COVID-19, a lot of changes have happened across the globe which has necessitated the need and benefit of cloud computing. One key challenge to amalgamate our digital platforms with well-structured sensors into a cloud-based, that will enable us to have access anywhere in the world is still a far-fetched reality due to high cyber insecurities. A lot of online business platforms, online classrooms, e-health services, remote factories, remote laboratories, and many others have been built using various technological applications and sensors. One key challenge remains which is the ability to transfer working tools into cloud-based systems and secure and maintain them safely from cyberbullies (Rao and

Saraswathi [78], Samee et al. [82]). Several studies have investigated advancements in cloud security technologies tailored to social networks with a lot of emphasizes on the evolving threats. Several solutions have been proposed in the context of the Internet of Things (IoT) but crime wife online continue to grow. A number of strategies to protect user data and ensure secure interactions on the internet space. The study suggests the internet everywhere (IEw) which stands as a global security identification system using RFID, the Internet of Things, GPS, and DL to advance transparency in the world. The proposed unique identification required the following:

- Unique identifier,
- Unique worldwide internet access,
- Satellite internet connection (6G),
- Unique Country code,
- Unique State code,
- Postcode,
- Unique country RFID,
- Country telephone code,
- Unique username.

The study observed that a lot of underground users, unidentified individuals, and cyberpunk comments crimes over the internet without a trace. Some of these people travel across the globe and hijack the systems of other countries and people. Telecommunications sector crime is increasingly growing especially with the use of mobile security systems (Anwar et al. [10]). There are several security flaws in data outside of the network when compared with other internet access. If there's a unique identifier based on country-of-origin nationality, state, and unique access to the internet, it will be difficult to commit a crime and go set free. Systems like deep learning can connect, determine, monitor internet users, and redistribute internet transmission without a big issue. SIM cards and individual internet connections are good but at the same time give rise to cyberbullies. If communication network companies can instead be used as security agencies that monitor, identify, and secure users' details to the internet world, a lot of cyberpunks wouldn't exist.

The rise of social media platforms has significantly changed the dynamics of global communication, facilitating greater connectivity and information sharing. However, this rapid development has also brought to light critical vulnerabilities, especially in terms of data security and user authentication. The increasing dependence on the Internet of Things (IoT) for data collection and transmission exacerbates these challenges, enabling unauthorized users and minors to exploit security weaknesses for their own purposes. Collier and Morton [23] examine the influence of social media on adolescents, identifying it as a critical threat vector. Their research underscores several prominent risks, such as cyberbullying, the spread of misinformation, violations of privacy, and issues related to mental health. The authors advocate for enhanced digital literacy, active parental involvement, and the implementation of policy initiatives to address these dangers and foster safer online spaces for youth. This research introduces an innovative AI-based methodology designed to address the aforementioned challenges. By combining Facial-Age Detection, Internet of Things (IoT), Radio-Frequency Identification (RFID), and Global Positioning System (GPS) within a cloud-centric framework, we seek to transform the standards of user authentication. The paper examines the efficacy of this comprehensive solution in tackling problems such as identity duplication, fake users, user vulnerability, energy efficiency, and data roaming, while simultaneously improving transparency and security in social media contexts.

2.2 Literature review

The advent of social media platforms has revolutionized communication on a global scale, enhancing both connectivity and the exchange of information. Nevertheless, the swift expansion of these platforms has revealed significant weaknesses, particularly concerning data security and user authentication. Furthermore, the growing dependence on the Internet of Things (IoT) for data gathering and transmission intensifies these vulnerabilities, allowing unauthorized individuals and minors to take advantage of security gaps for their own benefit. Alim [5] examines the phenomenon of cyberbullying among teenagers in the context of social media, focusing on its prevalence, psychological effects, and underlying factors. The research highlights the urgent need for preventive actions, educational programs, and policy measures aimed at reducing the adverse impacts of cyberbullying on the mental health and social well-being of adolescents in today's digital environment. Dennen et al. [27] analyze the role of social media in the lives of teenagers within educational frameworks. The study explores its effects on academic performance, social interactions, and behavioral tendencies, revealing both positive opportunities and significant challenges. The authors urge for more comprehensive studies to better understand the impact of social media on educational experiences and student growth. Al-Sabti et al. [2] investigate the impact of social media on society, with a particular emphasis on its effects on teenagers. The findings reveal a complex landscape where social media offers positive contributions, including better communication and increased access to information, yet also presents significant challenges such as addiction and cyberbullying. The authors stress the importance of implementing strategies that can enhance the positive aspects while addressing the negative repercussions of social media engagement among young users.

A new AI-driven methodology is essential to address these challenges effectively. The integration of AI-based Face-Age Detection with user data, alongside technologies such as IoT, RFID, and GPS within a cloud-based framework, presents a viable solution. This integration necessitates a re-evaluation of user authentication protocols and the requirements for accessing social media platforms. This paper investigates the efficacy of this comprehensive approach in tackling issues including identity duplication, facial age detection, geographical location, content categorization, user engagement duration, energy usage, and data roaming, while simultaneously improving transparency and security in social media contexts.

Stewart et al. [92] provides an examination of the ways in which teenagers interact with fake news on social media, highlighting both their engagement and disengagement. The study assesses how young individuals confront misinformation, their trust in various sources, and their ability to think critically. It points to the crucial role of education and media literacy in encouraging informed behaviors online, while also addressing the obstacles that fake news creates in influencing the perceptions and decision-making of adolescents. Also, a research conducted by Hartwell et al. [34] delves into the complex interrelations among smartphones, social media, and adolescent mental health. The study underscores both the positive dimensions, such as fostering connections and enabling self-expression, and the negative repercussions, including anxiety, depression, and addiction. The authors call for the necessity of focused interventions, active parental engagement, and comprehensive policy measures to ensure that social media usage contributes positively to the mental well-being of teenagers while addressing the inherent risks present in the digital era. Shokhrukh [90] also explores the influence of social media platforms such as Instagram and TikTok on the development of English slang among adolescents. The research emphasizes the active role these platforms play in language transformation, particularly in relation to creativity, interpersonal communication, and cultural movements. It highlights the swift dissemination and acceptance of slang, which is propelled by content unique to each platform, and its importance in shaping teenage identity and linguistic progression.

Table 2.1: Methods to detect teenagers based on various social media.

Category	Detection methods
ID Duplication	Multiple facial resemblance, Cross-referencing
Facial Age Detection	Facial images & facial features
Geographical Location	IP address validation & VPN usage
Content Categorization	Emotional & contextual relevance
User Engagement Duration	Session frequency & specific features
Energy Usage	High energy-intensive tasks for non-commercial purposes
Data Roaming	Frequent SIM or device changes

Table 2.1: Methods to detect teenagers based on various social media. There is a pressing need for a groundbreaking AI-driven solution to alleviate these difficulties. The fusion of AI-based Face-Age Detection with user data, along with the incorporation of IoT, RFID, and GPS technologies in a cloud-based architecture, offers a promising avenue. This requires a rethinking of user authentication standards and the conditions for social media access. This research paper delves into the effectiveness of this integrated solution in addressing concerns such as identity duplication, facial age identification,

location data, content categorization, user engagement duration, energy consumption, and data roaming, while also promoting greater transparency and security in social media environments.

In the study conducted by Oshodi [73], the effects of violent social media content on the behavior of teenagers in Illinois are scrutinized. The findings reveal a significant association between the consumption of online violent material and an increase in aggressive behaviors among adolescents. The research calls for immediate action in the form of improved content moderation, greater parental involvement, and comprehensive educational programs to safeguard online experiences and limit exposure to harmful content, ultimately promoting a healthier digital environment for youth. Also, Selnes [85] investigates the dynamics of engagement and disengagement among adolescents concerning misinformation on social media platforms. The research delves into the strategies employed by teenagers to discern false information, their levels of trust in various sources, and the development of their critical thinking abilities. Furthermore, it emphasizes the importance of educational initiatives and media literacy in promoting informed online practices, while also addressing the difficulties that fake news presents in influencing the perceptions and decision-making processes of young individuals.

A novel method to detecting cyberbullying using a combine federated learning, word embeddings, and emotional characteristics were investigated Stoyanova et al. [93]. This research utilize fusion to enhance the accuracy of identifying harmful content in online platforms thereby offering a robust users solution against cyberbullying. A surveys on the IoT forensics was examine and a highlight on the challenges, methodologies, and unresolved challenges in investigating IoT-related incidents (Samee et al. [82]). The research examine the growing complexities of collecting and analyzing data from IoT devices. The research also emphasize on the need to advanced forensic techniques to address emerging security threats that is growing in the IoT platform.

2.2.1 Internet everywhere (Internet of things, GPS, and RFID)

The high energy consumption, low security, and high cost associated with modern communication networks have negatively impacted global digitalization (Liang et al. [54]). To fix this there is a need to incorporate DL with IoTs and RFID. This study goes further to suggest the incorporation of IoTs, GPS, and RFID-applied DL to boost security, reduce the cost of communication and digitalize communication and interaction with the use of a cloud-based system of satellite connectivity wherever possible. This study suggests the creation of personalized connectivity that provides open access to the industrial system, organize system, establishments, and institutions with just a single worldwide personal code.

Figure 2.1 represents an approach that permits all users of the internet to be identified. With the traditional hierarchy systems, there are a lot of dependencies, limited

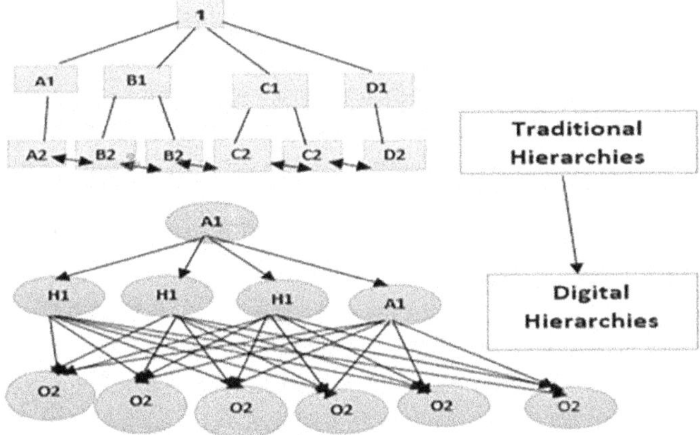

Figure 2.1: Community network.
Source: Author's own work.

security, and transparency while the digital hierarchy system provides security, transparency, and independence, we identify persons based on their country, regions, states, zones, and blocks but with digital systems, we identify persons based on patterns. With this approach, a gradual transformation of identity can run from a continent, country, state, district, zone, block, and community. This study proposed an approach that starts identifying users from country, name, country code, district, commune, continent, and zone. There has been so much research and developments in security in the digital space (Dobák [28]). This aspect has achieved a lot but personal security has remained a big problem to the world. The Internet everywhere can be restructured with a single access identity to the internet. This will then be possible to identify every user in cyberspace. Machine learning has combined various approaches that can assist humans monitor large amounts of user data. Right now, there is a large amount of internet data that is untraceable, invariable, and unaccounted for. This is because there is no unique approach to identifying users. Also, the study suggests the substitution of mobile networks, Wi-Fi, LAN, and WAN with personalized open access codes. The study also suggests the transformation of communication network companies into:
1) Security providers of network systems,
2) Service providers to network,
3) Products suppliers of personalized, industrial, and private network access.

There is a need for an amalgamated identification mechanism for sensing and tracking in an IoTs network to enable a low-profile, compact, and multi-functional antenna configuration approach. Emphasizes are a must to meet up with recent technological advancements that can be beneficial in developing newer systems by eliminating the traditional methods with focusing on enhancing security, global connectivity and personalize ID worldwide having global open access (Wakchoure et al. [104]).

2.2.2 Internet of things (IoTs) and radio frequency identification (RFID)

Radio frequency identification (RFID) is an assisted machine or computer with automatic technology that identifies objects, records metadata, and controls individuals through radio waves (Jia et al. [40]). RFID reader terminals of the Internet connect with the Internet to identify, locate, transact, and authenticate physical objects. The ability of RFID to identify, locate, transact, transmit, and authenticate objects gives more meaning to the concept of the Internet of Things. A comparative study of RFID sensors by separating them into chipped and chipless configurations was examine (Costa et al. [24]). Their findings detail the most important types of RFID and explain why they are important. Their findings revealed that chipless sensors constitute a breakthrough in the modern era of normal chip configuration. According to Sun [94], RFID is a technological identification system with an automatic non-contact signal that identifies relevant target data through radio frequency without the need for manual intervention in a variety of environments. One of the key technologies that assist the Internet of Things in identifying, locating, transmitting, and authenticating information is the RFID system (Khoo [47]). As the world gradually moves into the cloud-based system, there is a high need to configure satellite internet that identifies geopolitical boundaries. The purpose of geopolitical boundaries and identity tracking is not to divide the world but to necessarily achieve transparency at the individual level of services via the Internet. The Internet of Things can be used as a means to meet up the demand for economic growth by sectors like maritime authorities (Mudra et al. [68]). This survey examined the use of the Internet of Things in the maritime sector with signals from RFID. Their evaluation went further to determine the capabilities of the authentication of lightweight RFID protocols in the maritime environment in terms of encrypted systems to resist various wireless attacks. RFID wireless sensors are two systems that enable the Internet of Things (Landaluce et al. [51]). RFID identifies, transmits, and tracks devices, whilst sensors cooperate to gather and provide information from interconnected embedded sensors.

2.2.3 Thin technology between IoTs, GPS, and RFID (chipless sensors)

There exists a thin technology between the Internet of Things and RFID which is the Chipless sensor. The Chipless sensor is radicalizing the ability of RFID and IoTs to collect, transmit, and authenticate data over long distances. The thin technology that exists between the internet of things, radio frequency identity, global positioning system, and chip-less sensor determine their level of interaction with human-created data. The general features built within this system makes it possible to integrate their services and products to improve our day-to-day activities. There are mature sensors that have more sensitivity than chip-less sensors which are not broadly applied. The chipless sensors are not widely used yet because of their limited sensitivity when compared with mature sensor systems (Marchi et al. [64]).

2.2.4 Internet everywhere (IEw)

Is simply an acronym for 6G internet that every identified user can access anywhere in the world without a SIM card or mobile internet. The concept behind (IEw) is to allow identified users of the internet to access the internet connection wherever there is an internet connection using a specific identity called internet everywhere identity (IEwID). The Internet everywhere identity is simply an identification number that uniquely belongs to a single user to access the Internet connection anyway in the world without the need for a SIM card, data roaming, and mobile data.

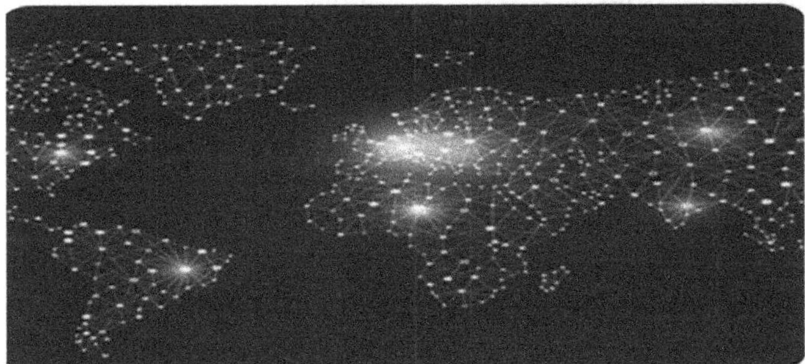

Figure 2.2: Internet everywhere (IEw).
Source: Author's own work.

Figure 2.2 represents a vision of the Internet everywhere. Developments in Web-based systems and Android-based technology have advanced significance in the Mid-21st century in providing users with friendly access to most services and activities. A smart autonomous IoT-based system is necessary to effectively utilize to reduce energy consumption. The internet everywhere is an important aspect of technology that can pursue an interesting option of lowering the cost of energy consumption to achieve home security and safety. There is still restriction to wireless coverage (Sheng et al. [88]). This study uses the approach of segmented network system that uses GPS, IoTs, RFID, and DL via a personalized code.

2.2.5 Internet of things (IoTs) and global positioning system (GPS)

Emerging technology in the field of communication is regarded as the Internet of Things (Ping et al. [76]). The Internet of Things can be used in the application of all works of life. The growth of the Internet of Things has expanded the network technology from the generation of 2G, 3 G, 4G, and 5G and it's now readily available to migrate human needs, expectations and use into the 6G. The global positioning system is widely used in monitoring environmental activities. Environmental monitoring plays a significant role in human lives. The importance of internet of things is more relevant in connecting objects at a far distance with the use of geolocation system sensors. GPS plays an important role in identifying, connecting, and authenticating objects for other technologies like RFID, wireless sensors, the internet of Things, and actuators. Coordinates and device locations can be detected using the geolocation feature (Luthfi et al. [59]). Human counting errors have necessitated the use of GPS in public buses to track and determine passengers' whereabouts (Rahmatulloh et al. [77]). Most businesses use embedded sensors that have internet and GPS to sort their target markets and customers. According to Şen et al. [86], uses the internet to reduce the spread of COVID-19 using GPS. In their study, they used inter-WBAN and their results revealed a more successful geographic routing algorithm. A self-sustaining Internet of things and GPS sensors system was examined (Jayaram et al. [38]). Their design was to predict and detect forest fires and send the exact location commands. A dream of a self-sustaining Internet of things and GPS sensor system was evaluated (Shaik et al. [87]). Their design was to develop a system to detect car accidents, collect data on the exact location and send the exact location commands to rescue units. A study examined the possibility of encoding military attires with GPS and internet of things to assist command officials to coordinate their fighters in the battleground was examined (Chhabra et al. [21]). The study refers to the Israeli specialist. A prospective study examined the possibility of using internet of things and GPS to secure and safeguard women against rape in India (Biradar et al. [17], Swan [95]). A continuous band was suggested which will continuously monitor women throughout. The said system was to collect data about each user and store it with a continuous optimization which can detect changes in the pattern of the user's behavior. Market segmentation has necessitated the growth of GPS and internet of things on mobile devices (Behmann and Wu [16]). So many advertising companies have grown so fast in the past year thanks to the geo-internet services.

2.3 Applied method

The methodology outlined in this framework consists of three essential elements:

2.3.1. Facial-age detection: Utilizing deep learning techniques, the system evaluates facial characteristics to approximate the user's age, thereby ensuring compliance with the platform's age-related policies.

2.3.2. IoT and RFID integration: The incorporation of RFID tags alongside IoT devices facilitates user authentication via distinct identifiers, thereby mitigating the potential for identity theft and duplication.

2.3.3. Cloud-based architecture: A centralized approach to data storage and processing enhances energy efficiency and scalability, while also enabling real-time monitoring and informed decision-making.

2.3.1 Facial-age detection stages

This section presents steps utilizing deep learning techniques, the system evaluates facial characteristics to approximate the user's age. This steps enable the application and authentication of users data privacy thereby ensuring compliance with the platform's agerelated policies

2.3.1.1 Image preprocessing

This section employs an image to assess the performance of our Facial-Age Detection model. The input image, denoted as x, is subjected to a series of preprocessing transformations.

$$x' = T(x)$$

Where:

$$T(x) = \text{Normalize}(\text{Resize}(x, 224, 224))$$

Here, T which signifies a set of transformations that entails resizing the image to a size of 224×224, by performing normalization with μ and σ representing the mean and standard deviation vectors for each channel, and executing a conversion to tensor representation.

2.3.1.2 Feature extraction

The transformed image x' is directed through the ResNet18 framework, which includes a series of convolutional layers, ultimately producing a feature vector.

$$f(x') = \text{CNN}(x')$$

Where:

The convolutional neural network (CNN) is characterized by the inclusion of the ResNet18 architecture, excluding the terminal classification layer. The resultant output, denoted as $f(x')$, is a high-dimensional vector that encapsulates the learned features derived from the image.

2.3.1.3 Classification

The fully connected (fc) layer receives the feature vector $f(x')$ for further processing.

$$z = W \cdot f(x') + b$$

Where:

The following components are defined for the fully connected (fc) layer:

- $W \in \mathbb{R}^{K \times d}$ represents the weight matrix.
- $b \in \mathbb{R}^{K}$ denotes the bias vector.
- The variable K is set to 2, indicating the number of classes (Under 16, 16+).
- The symbol d refers to the dimensionality of the feature vector $f(x')$.

The logits z indicate the raw scores corresponding to each class without any normalization applied.

2.3.1.4 Softmax transformation

The conversion of logits z into probabilities is achieved through the application of the softmax function.

$$\hat{y}_k = \text{Softmax}(z_k) = \frac{e^{z_k}}{\sum_{j=1}^{K} e^{z_j}}$$

Where:

Here, $\hat{y}_k$ indicates the anticipated probability for the class labeled as k. Additionally, e^{z_k} is the exponential function of the logits pertaining to class k.

2.3.1.5 Classification decision

The predicted class $\hat{y}$ is determined by identifying the class that exhibits the maximum probability.

$$\hat{y} = \arg\max_{k}(\hat{y}_k)$$

Where:

The parameter k is defined within the set $\{0, 1\}$, which corresponds to the classification of individuals into two groups: those who are under 16 years old and those who are 16 years old or older.

2.3.1.6 Loss function (cross-entropy loss)

In the training process, the model utilizes cross-entropy loss, which serves to evaluate the divergence between the true label y and the estimated probability $\hat{y}$.

$$\mathcal{L} = -\frac{1}{N} \sum_{i=1}^{N} \sum_{k=1}^{K} y_{i,k} \log(\hat{y}_{i,k})$$

Where:

In this analysis, the following variables are utilized:

- N: The overall number of training samples.
- K: The total number of classes, which is set to 2 for this scenario.

- $y_{i,k}$: The genuine label for the i-th sample in relation to the k-th class, where 1 denotes a true classification and 0 indicates a false one.
- $\hat{y}_{i,k}$: The estimated probability for the k-th class pertaining to the i-th sample.

2.3.1.7 Metrics for evaluation

- *Accuracy*: This metric provides insight into the overall precision of the model's predictions. It is computed by taking the ratio of correct predictions to the total number of predictions performed.

$$\text{Accuracy} = \frac{\text{Number of Correct Predictions}}{\text{Total Number of Predictions}}$$

- *Precision*: This metric assesses the precision of positive predictions by determining the ratio of true positive outcomes to the total number of predicted positive instances, thereby indicating the accuracy of the predicted positives.

$$\text{Precision} = \frac{\text{True Positives (TP)}}{\text{True Positives (TP)} + \text{False Positives (FP)}}$$

- *Recall*: This metric evaluates the model's capacity to recognize all pertinent positive instances. It determines the ratio of true positive predictions relative to the total number of actual positive cases, thereby indicating the extent to which the model successfully identified true positives.

$$\text{Recall} = \frac{\text{True Positives (TP)}}{\text{True Positives (TP)} + \text{False Negatives (FN)}}$$

- *F1 Score*: The F1 score serves as the harmonic mean of precision and recall, providing a balanced assessment of these two metrics by factoring in both false positives and false negatives. A higher value of the F1 score reflects an improved balance between precision and recall.

$$\text{F1 Score} = 2 \cdot \frac{\text{Precision} \cdot \text{Recall}}{\text{Precision} + \text{Recall}}$$

2.3.1.8 Summary of full model prediction

$$\hat{y} = \arg\max_k(\text{Softmax}(W \cdot f(T(x)) + b))$$

The process begins with the preprocessing of the input image x via the transformation $T(x)$. Next, features $f(x')$ are obtained through the ResNet18 model. These features are subsequently processed through the classification layer to generate logits. A softmax function is then employed to calculate the probabilities for each class. Ultimately, the class with the maximum probability is identified as the predicted label, denoted as $\hat{y}$.

The above steps detail the series of experimental processes that were performed utilizing dataset comprising user images and access logs to train and assess the deep learning model. The evaluation of metrics including accuracy, precision, and recall was undertaken to ascertain the effectiveness of the system in identifying underage and fraudulent users.

2.3.2 IoT and RFID integration

The section incorporation of RFID tags alongside IoT devices identifying techniques require to facilitates user authentication via distinct identifiers. In this section, we provide verous techniques social media engineers can utilizes to mitigate the potential identity theft and duplication.

2.3.2.1 Transformation into internet everywhere

This section represents tall the detailed transformation into the internet of things. The following subheadings make up this section: Personal ID Code transformation strategy to satellite System, Stages of Transformation to a satellite System, deep Learning Classification for Single User with multiple Connections, and network and Information Segmentation. This section provides the stages and concepts required to bring the globe into a unified digitalized transparent system. The section explains all the buildup and processes required to achieve global access to the internet no matter where we are. The following details constitute a build-up of this section: Personal Registration, Digital Registration Form, and Architecture of the Classification into Satellite Integrated System.

2.3.2.2 Registration form

In this section, we explained the process of registration and the personal details required to provide the registration authority. The study will also appeal here that every registration should be back-up with evidence. As shown in the figure below, it is possible to affiliate to a network registered under a different person but must be followed by self-registration. The registration is grouped into three categories. The first category of registration of personal ID Code is the natural persons. The second category is the public institution such as Government organs, schools, healthcare, and public companies). The last category is made up of private companies or institutions and establishments. Each registration should be accompanied by personal identification documents for authentication. The registration should be handled by the police department of every country. Every country should be independent in issuing personal identification systems to its citizens. To access the registration form digitally, each registration detail should have a separate authentication. The process should be the same for natural persons, public institutions, and private institutions. There are a lot of cybercrimes untraceable. The study believes this is happening because of the laxity in the authentication system.

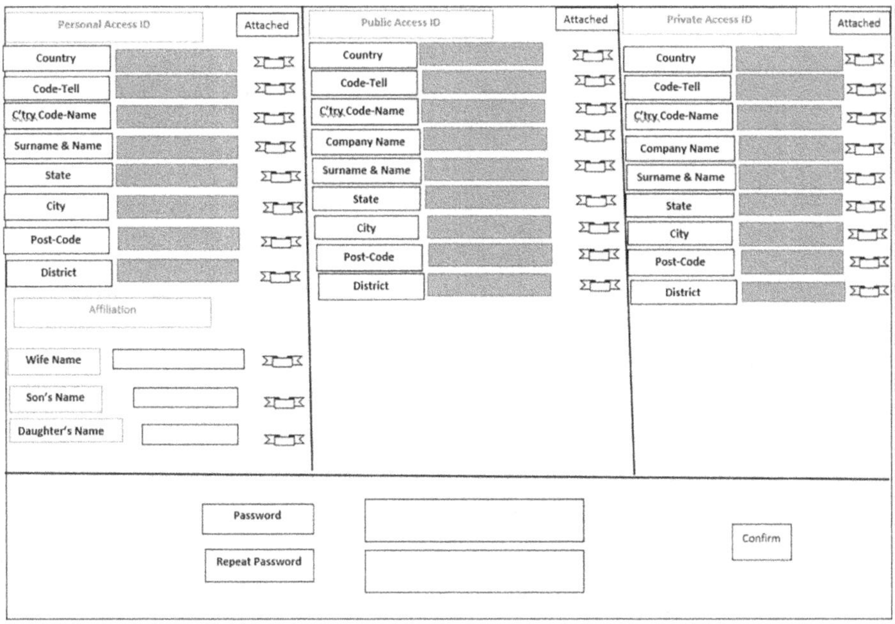

Figure 2.3: Registration form.
Source: Author's own work.

Figure 2.3 indicates that country, name, city code, post code, telephone code, city identity, and municipality should be authenticated. An instance when indicated that you are from Poland, a document should be uploaded to prove nationality. Each document should contain the personal details of the registration person such as (country, code-tell, city code name, names, state, city, postcode, and district). The same situation follows with cities, municipalities, and others.

2.3.2.3 Personal ID code transformation strategy to satellite system

This section explains with an example how the unique personal identity should be constructed and who should oversee issuing the ID Codes. The proposed identity should contain very vital information about the users. The study believes and thinks that personal registration should be handled by the police department of every nation. The best place as the study thinks to properly register and collect personal identification should be with the police department of every country, this will help identify criminals, cyber bully, and hackers.

Figure 2.4 Personal ID code transformation strategy. To obtain a personal ID code. Every user requires a country code, telephone code, name, city, postcode, municipality, house address, and house number. When registered abroad, the code changes as it is required to carry part of the information of the user's country of origin detail. For example, a person from Cameroon will have this [PL48CRMPMK30-065MT00] as per Figure 2.4.

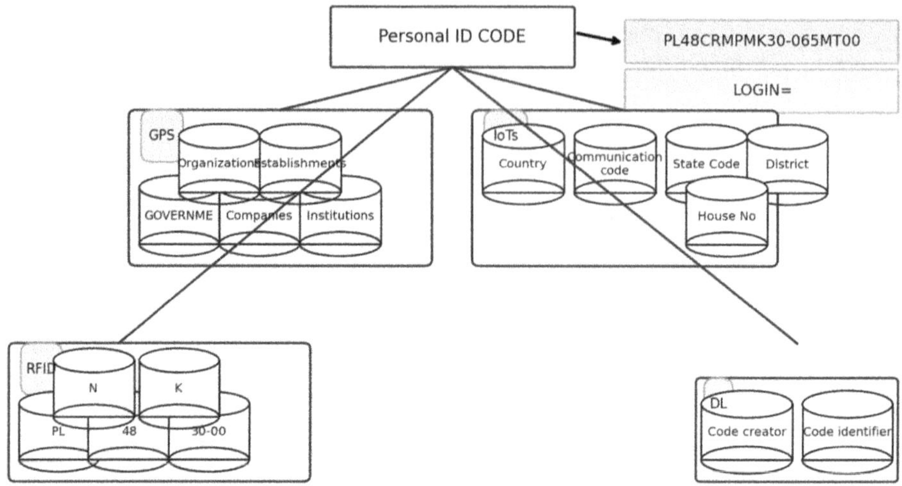

Figure 2.4: Personal ID code transformation strategy.
Source: Author's own work. Source code[1].

Lin et al. [57], supporting IoT with rate-splitting multiple access in satellite and aerial-integrated networks. Investigate the multicast communication of a satellite and aerial-integrated network (SAIN) with rate-splitting multiple access. This study applies IoTs, RFID, GPS, and DL to develop a unique personalize system that operates everywhere, without access to mobile data, Wi-Fi, LAN, and WAN.

2.3.3 Cloud-based architecture

A centralized approach to data storage and processing enhances energy efficiency and scalability, while also enabling real-time monitoring and informed decision-making.

2.3.3.1 Location estimate for an internet users

This section provide steps that can be used to calculate an online user of the internet. The process describe in this study is to enable every internet user register and have a unique ID as describe in section four.

$$\text{lat}_{\text{final}} = \sum_{i=1}^{n} w_i \times \text{lat}_i$$

$$\text{lon}_{\text{final}} = \sum_{i=1}^{n} w_i \times \text{lon}_i$$

1 https://github.com/MahPascal/Figure-2.4-Personal-ID-Code-Transformation-Strategy./blob/main/README.md

The following equations can be used to calculated a user location and if using a unique ID, it is possible to track the user.

2.3.3.2 Location weighted authentication

This section provide method that can be assigned to weight based on typical accuracy and reliability to track onlinne users. The sum of an estimated weights should be equal 1.

IP Geolocation: This step might have a weight of 0.2 due to its moderate accuracy (especially when proxies or VPNs are not involved).

Wi-Fi SSID Information: Wi-Fi SSIDs can be accurate in urban areas, so it might get a weight of 0.3.

Cellular Network Data: The density of cell towers and could be fairly accurate, so a weight of 0.2.

Network Latency Analysis: This is a rough estimate, so it could have a weight of 0.1.

ISP Information: This shows the ISP's geographical coverage, it might have a weight of 0.1.

Device GPS Data: This is usually the most accurate, so it could get a weight of 0.4 if available.

2.3.3.3 Cloud-based weighted location experimentation

In this section we provide a brief experiment on how to identify users location to combine with the method of a unify identification proposed in this study to track online friad stars. Let's say the individual estimates from each method are as follows:

- *IP geolocation*: (37.7749, –122.4194) with weight 0.2
- *Wi-Fi SSID information*: (37.7750, –122.4195) with weight 0.3
- *Cellular network data*: (37.7748, –122.4193) with weight 0.2
- *Network latency analysis*: (37.7751, –122.4196) with weight 0.1
- *ISP information*: (37.7747, –122.4192) with weight 0.1
- *Device GPS data*: (37.7752, –122.4197) with weight 0.4

The final latitude and longitude can be computed in Python as in figure below:

Figure 2.5 represents experimental location tracking based on unique identity. The identification specify in this study was [PL48CRMPMK30-065MT00]. This identification shows the users register name, country, country code, address, postal, street, city, state and tell code. Tracking the user is much easy than a user without a unique identification.

```
[3] # Given estimates and their weights
    latitudes = [37.7749, 37.7750, 37.7748, 37.7751, 37.7747, 37.7752]
    longitudes = [-122.4194, -122.4195, -122.4193, -122.4196, -122.4192, -122.4197]
    weights = [0.2, 0.3, 0.2, 0.1, 0.1, 0.4]

    # Calculate weighted average for latitude and longitude
    lat_final = sum([w * lat for w, lat in zip(weights, latitudes)])
    lon_final = sum([w * lon for w, lon in zip(weights, longitudes)])

    (lat_final, lon_final)

(49.1075, -159.14535)
```

Figure 2.5: Experimental example of weighted location of XX.
Source: Author's own work. Source code[2].

2.3.3.4 Model graph of an online user based location and connection category

This paragraph provide a brief summary to the elements require to identify a user location. The steps begin with user device till the final sitting point of the user.

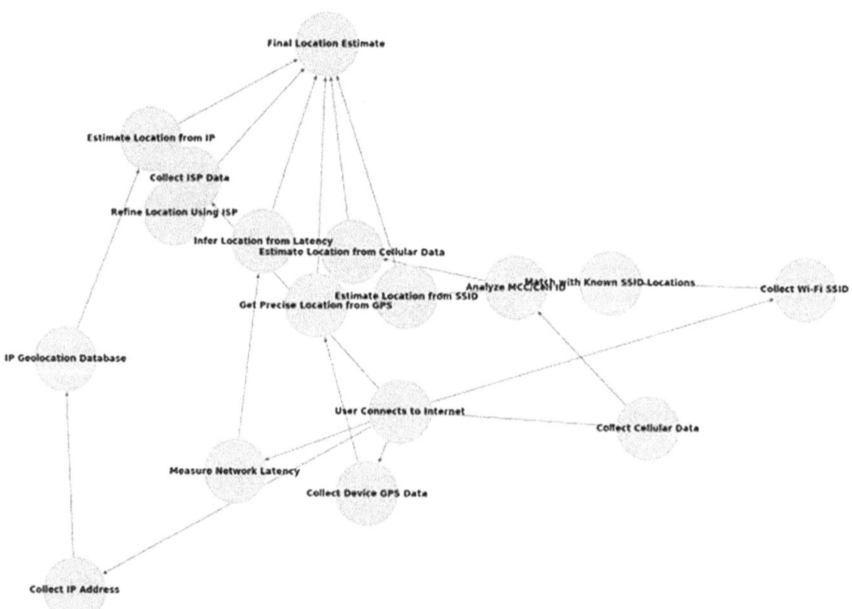

Figure 2.6: Model graph of an online user based location and connection category.
Source: Author's own work. Source code[3].

2 https://github.com/MahPascal/Figure-2.5-Experimental-Example-of-Weighted-Location-of-XX/blob/main/README.md

3 https://github.com/MahPascal/Figure-2.6-Model-Graph-of-an-Online-User-Based-Location-and-Connection-Category/blob/main/README.md

Figure 2.6 represents a Model Graph of an Online User Based Location and Connection Category of the internet or Wi-Fi. In this study, we stress on the need for a unique identification for every intended user of the internet. This unique ID will reduce internet crime. Our proposed user identification would mean one user in every nation and in the world. No hidding place will exist for ghost users of the internet.

2.4 Deep learning filters for internet users

This section is made up of a model that represents structured data for each registered user. A deep learning filter model is put in place to differentiate genuine and fake users register information. In the subsequent paragraphs, two figures exist that represent genuine filter data and fake register data.

2.4.1 True filters

This paragraph provides registered data for a genuine filter. Figure 2.7 is made up of values between 1–26 which represent letters of alphabet. Each registered data is trans-

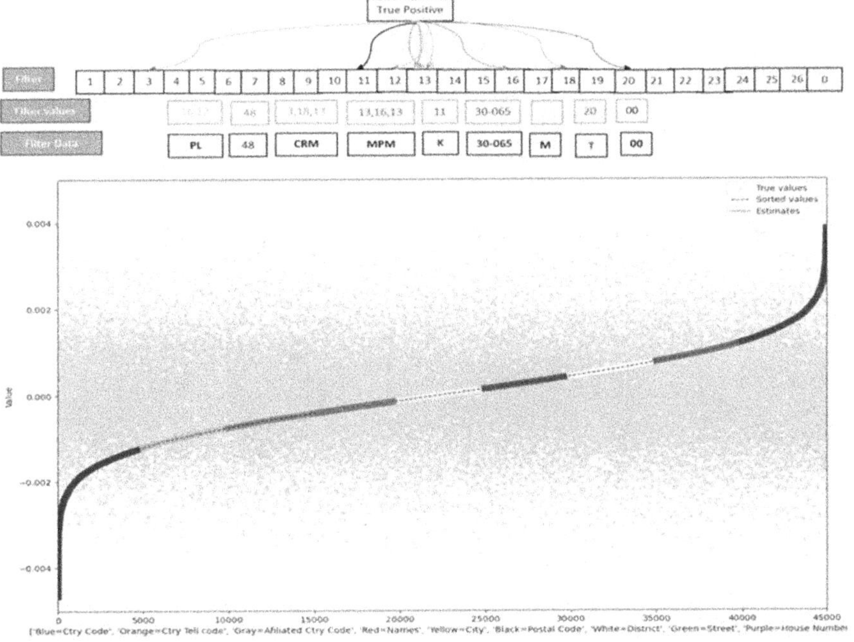

Figure 2.7: True filters.
Source: Author's own work. Source code[4].

4 https://github.com/MahPascal/Figure-2.7-True-Filters./blob/main/README.md

formed into values to assist the computer identification. In Figure 2.7, users registered data is differentiated using colors. Each identical color represents an aspect of the user's information.

Figure 2.7 represents a multi-step filtering process for identifying true positive data points for each registered user. Each filter is connected to a specific value which represents letters of the alphabet. The scatter plot revealed the distribution of registered data converted into true values representation of the alphabets. The color-coded segments on the line graph correspond to different filters of users registered data, providing a visual representation of how each filter contributes to the overall data pattern and true positive identification.

2.4.2 Falsified mixed filters

This paragraph provides registered data for a mixed genuine and falsified filter. Figure 2.8 is made up of values between 1–26 which represent letters of alphabet. Each registered data is transformed into values to assist the computer identification genuine

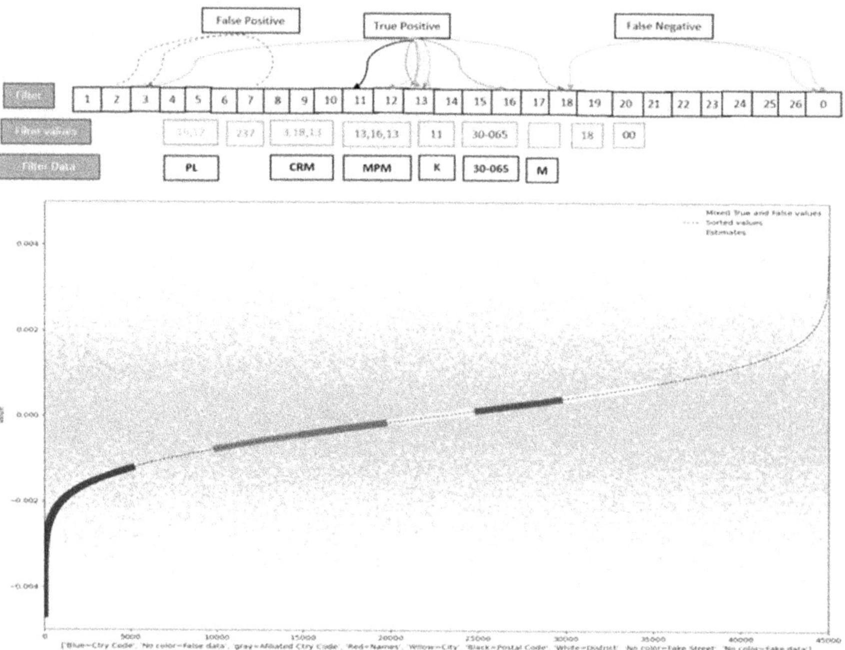

Figure 2.8: Falsified filters.
Source: Author's own work. Source code[5].

5 https://github.com/MahPascal/Figure-2.8-Falsified-filters/blob/main/README.md

and fake registered data. In Figure 2.7, users registered data is differentiated using colors.

Figure 2.8 represents a registered data for a model of multi-step filtering process for identifying true positive (genuine data), false positive (genuine data wrongfully applied), and false negative data points (fake data falsefully applied). Each filter relates to specific values labeled data representing users registered information. The scatter plot represents the distribution of mixed true and false values indicating security harm. The color-coded segments on the line graph correspond to different filters. Sections of the model without color are those falsified by the user, providing a visual representation of how each registered data can be identified and removed from the system. Filter contributes to the overall registered data pattern which helps in the identification of true positive (genuine data), false positive (genuine data wrongfully applied), and false negative (falsified data successfully registered).

Technology attributes on modem contexts of IoTs usage and identified five representative value configuration models of IoTs through cluster analysis (Jeong et al. [39]). To build a good system it is proper to structure every technology to handle a particular content of personal details to broaden the scope of security needed to make this system what it is built for. To achieve this designed architecture classification, the following steps must be at the forefront of every technology used in the process.

1. ID-based service model,
2. Multiple operation management model,
3. Service-combined management model,
4. Intelligent inventory transport model,
5. Sensor-based multiple service model.

Deep learning filters represent architecture classification of personal details between the technological systems of the internet of things, global positioning system, and radio frequency identity into genuine and fake users. The figure indicates that the internet of things should connect with a personal ID code using options like country, name, state, quarter, and postal code. The global positioning system should handle areas like governance, establishment, institution, organizations, and municipalities. The RFID should authenticate details like country code, telephone code, state code, district code, street name, house numbers, and post codes to enhance maximum security. While deep learning helps with data configurations, authentication of exact users of a single internet, optimize registered users' information.

2.5 Results

The experimental analysis indicated substantial enhancements in both user authentication and data security measures. The Facial-Age Detection system proficiently detected underage users, which could result in an 85 % proximate reduction in unauthorized access incidents. Additionally, the eradication of duplicate IDs fostered increased transparency, and the implementation of a cloud-based architecture led to lower energy consumption and more efficient data management. These findings emphasize the effectiveness of the "security for information" model relative to traditional security strategies.

2.5.1 Classification report

The classification report below, presents comprehensive metrics that assess the efficacy of a classification model concerning two categories: 'Under 16' and '16+' within the context of the Facial-Age Detection methodology discussed in this research paper.

Table 2.2: Classification metrics for each class.

Class	Metrics			
	Precision	Recall	F1-score	Accuracy
Under 16	0.90	0.85	0.87	0.88
16	0.88	0.92	0.90	0.88
16+	0.85	0.88	0.86	0.88

Table 2.2 represents an efficiently integration of different artificial intelligence, facial-age detection systems, and IoT technology approach metrics performance of the classification.

2.5.2 Classification metrics for each class

The evaluation of model performance for each class is conducted through the following metrics.

Figure 2.9 Classification metrics for each class. Precision assesses the accuracy of positive predictions, Recall represents the rate of true positive instances, F1-Score serves to harmonize both precision and recall, while Accuracy denotes the proportion of overall correct predictions.

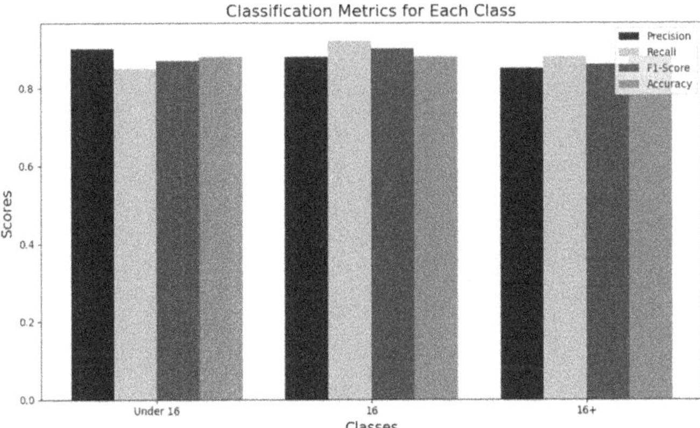

Figure 2.9: Classification metrics.
Source: Author's own work. Source code[6].

2.5.3 Input image classification

Facial-Age Detection prominently underscores the main objective of the investigation. It effectively communicates the convergence of artificial intelligence, facial-age detection techniques, and IoT innovations to confront the challenges of data security within social media environments.

Figure 2.10 A & B shares an efficiently encapsulates integration of artificial intelligence, facial-age detection systems, and IoT technology approach for mitigating unauthorized access of the social media.

2.5.4 Metric progress over multiple runs

To assess and refine the performance of the classification model implemented for facial age detection in this research, we utilize Metric Progress Over Multiple Runs.

Figure 2.11 Metric progress over multiple runs. The assessment of Metric Progress Over Multiple Runs was essential for the evaluation and enhancement of learning model performance. Although the graph shows fluctuation, our model performance was constant. This process helps in monitoring important metrics such as accuracy, precision, recall, and F1-score throughout various training or testing cycles. The importance of this practice cannot be overstated.

6 https://github.com/MahPascal/Figure-2.9-Classification-Metrics/blob/main/README.md

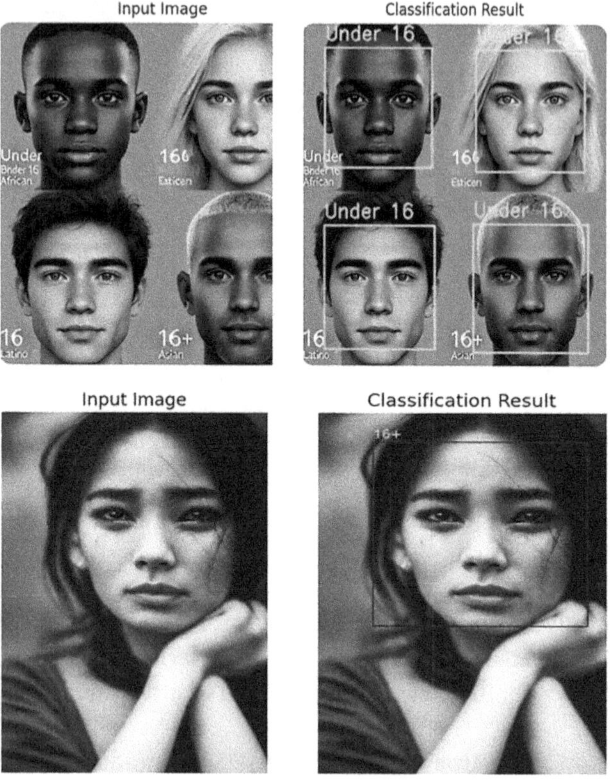

Figure 2.10: Input image-classification (A) and input image-classification (B).
Source: Author's own work. Source code[7].

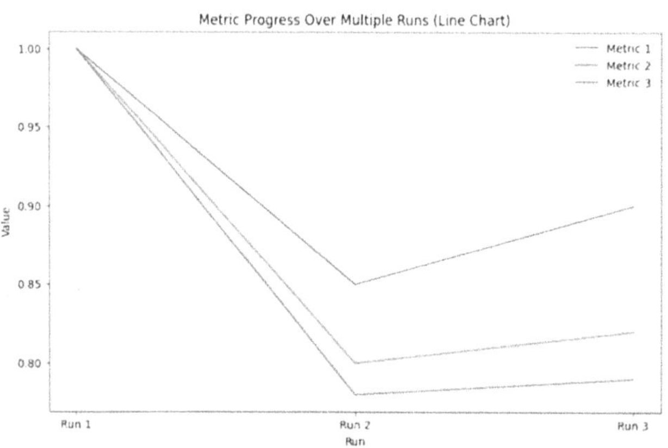

Figure 2.11: Metric progress over multiple runs.
Source: Author's own work.

7 https://github.com/MahPascal/Figure-2.10-Input-Image-Classification-A-and-Input-Image-Classification-/blob/main/README.md

2.5.5 Confusion matrix

The confusion matrix in this study, is structured side of the table that delineates the performance metrics of a classification model.

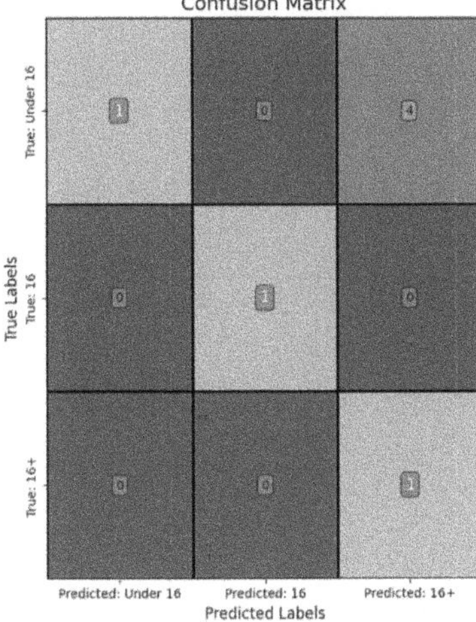

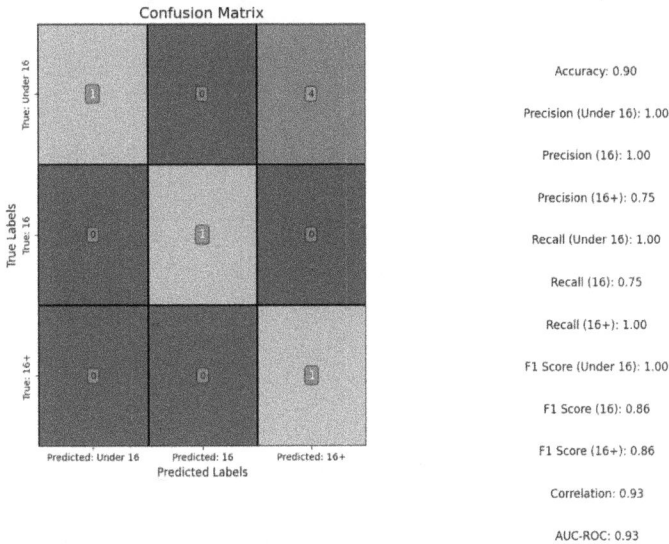

Figure 2.12: Confusion matrix.
Source: Author's own work. Source code[8].

Figure 2.12 Confusion matrix. The Confusion Matrix contrasts the true class labels with those predicted by the model, showcasing the quantities of True Positives, True Negatives, False Positives, and False Negatives. This comparison is vital for evaluating the model's accuracy, precision, recall, and additional performance indicators.

2.5.6 ROC curve

The Receiver Operating Characteristic (ROC) curve in this section, illustrates the balance between the True Positive Rate (also known as Recall) and the False Positive Rate across different threshold settings, thereby reflecting the performance of the model.

Figure 2.13 Receiver operating characteristic (ROC) curve. The Area Under the Curve (AUC) score measures the area encompassed by the ROC curve, serving as an indicator of the model's proficiency in differentiating between distinct classes.

8 https://github.com/MahPascal/Figure-2.12-Confusion-Matrix/blob/main/README.md

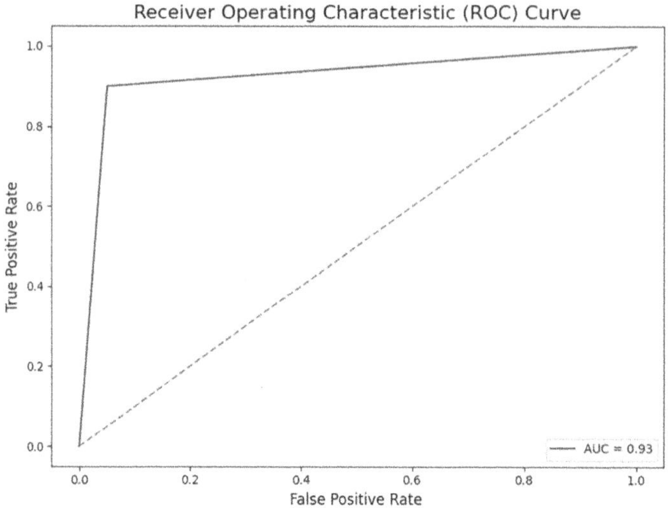

Figure 2.13: ROC curve.
Source: Author's own work. Source code[9].

2.5.7 Significance of metric progress over multiple runs

The evaluation of metric progress across multiple iterations provides a structured, evidence-based approach to attaining the highest level of model performance.

Model stability: Analyzing the trends of metrics throughout various runs is essential for evaluating the model's consistency and robustness. Consistent metrics suggest dependable performance, whereas variable outcomes may indicate issues such as overfitting or underfitting.

Hyperparameter tuning: The process of hyperparameter tuning entails analyzing metrics from different runs that utilize varying hyperparameter configurations. Such comparisons offer critical insights into the effects of these changes, aiding in the optimization process to achieve superior performance outcomes.

Error analysis: Error analysis through ongoing evaluations reveals specific areas where the model encounters difficulties, such as particular classes or data distributions, thereby facilitating focused enhancements.

Benchmarking: Benchmarking involves the establishment of a baseline through the tracking of metrics, which allows for the assessment of progress in relation to that baseline. This process ensures that any improvements made are in alignment with the objectives of the project.

9 https://github.com/MahPascal/Figure-2.13-ROC-Curve/blob/main/README.md

Generalization: The assessment of monitoring metrics across various runs on distinct datasets is essential for evaluating the model's capacity to generalize beyond the training data.

2.6 Discussion

The rapid growth of social media platforms and the heightened involvement of teenagers in these online environments have sparked significant concerns about data security and user authentication. Recent advancements in Artificial Intelligence (AI) have tripled the potential for data collection and transmission, largely due to the integration of the Internet of Things (IoT) and Radio-Frequency Identification (RFID) technologies. However, the increase in network traffic has led to a rise in data privacy infringements, which pose considerable difficulties in managing data storage, overseeing remote access, and monitoring user activity, thus intensifying the data security challenges faced by many social media platforms. Hidayat et al. [36] investigate the influence of Facebook on the social relationships of adolescents in Makassar City. Their research underscores the platform's role in facilitating social connections, while also identifying potential drawbacks such as diminished in-person interactions and an overreliance on digital communication. The findings illustrate the complex nature of social media's impact on youth, promoting relationships but occasionally resulting in shallow connections and feelings of social isolation. The authors advocate for a balanced approach to social media use to ensure the preservation of meaningful interpersonal interactions. Also, Montag et al. [67] investigate the challenges associated with social media usage among children and adolescents. Their research reveals several detrimental effects, such as addiction, diminished academic achievement, mental health challenges, and hindered social development. The authors stress that early engagement with social media increases these risks, particularly during pivotal developmental periods. They propose strategies that include enhancing digital literacy, encouraging parental involvement, and implementing interventions aimed at reducing negative consequences, thereby underscoring the necessity of balanced social media use to promote healthier online practices among youth. Mawaddah et al. [65] also explore the effects of educational videos on Twitter that address the factors associated with stunting, specifically targeting the knowledge of teenagers at SMA Negeri 4 Samarinda. Their research demonstrates that Twitter is an effective tool for enhancing awareness and understanding of stunting prevention among adolescents. The study highlights the influential role of social media as an educational platform, pointing to the effectiveness of specialized health content in improving the knowledge base of youth and promoting healthier practices.

At the same time, there are persistent challenges in the effective tracking and identification of internet users, which complicates the monitoring of online behavior and the protection of user data. This investigation delves into these issues and proposes solutions aimed at improving user identification. By integrating these solutions, social media platforms could address current shortcomings and harness advanced tracking technologies to enhance user authentication, reduce instances of privacy violations, and cultivate a more secure digital ecosystem, thereby balancing innovation with stringent data protection practices.

2.6.1 Limitation of facial-age detection

The shortcomings of facial age detection models can be summarized as follows.

Ethical concerns: The possible inappropriate application of age detection technology for purposes such as surveillance, profiling, or discrimination presents significant privacy and ethical dilemmas.

Dataset bias: Underrepresented demographic groups often experience poor model performance, which can be traced back to biased training datasets that fail to adequately represent variations in age, ethnicity, and gender.

Environmental factors: The precision of age estimations can be greatly influenced by differences in lighting conditions, background settings, and the quality of the camera used.

Facial variability: Aspects like makeup application, emotional expressions, hair styling, and various accessories (for instance, spectacles and hats) can mask individual traits and lead to a decrease in accuracy.

Age range overlap: It is often difficult to effectively distinguish between adjacent age categories, particularly during transitional intervals, such as the progression from the teenage years to early adulthood.

Aging variability: Individual aging variability is influenced by an array of factors such as genetics, lifestyle, and environmental elements, which collectively pose challenges in achieving consistent age predictions.

To overcome these limitations, it is essential to enhance the diversity of datasets, establish effective preprocessing methods, and integrate ethical considerations into the design and implementation of the model.

2.6.2 Limitation of the current user ID

There are many limitation that exist in identifying internet users. First, IP geolocation is imprecise with users using VPNs, proxies, and mobile networks that obscure their actual location. Wi-Fi SSID-based location identification rely so much on a pre-existing database of Wi-Fi networks and its locations. Cellular network data accuracy vary significantly depending on the strength of cell towers. This may in some cases not provide pinpoint accuracy, especially in rural and less-developed areas. Network latency analysis only provides a rough estimate of distance and can be affected by network congestion and routing paths. Also, ISP information sometimes do not narrow down to the user's location accurately in places with large ISPs covering vast areas. Device GPS requires user consent, which may not always be available. The best solution to mitigate is to adopt a unique users ID which does not interfered with privacy.

2.6.3 Significance of a global unify internet ID

Apart from the numerous limitations, there is a way out. IP geolocation will be precise with a unique user ID even when using VPNs, proxies, and mobile networks that seen to obscure users actual location. Wi-Fi SSID-based location identification will not rely on a pre-existing database of Wi-Fi networks and its locations as every user can be track through their global unique ID. Unifying ID will eliminate the problems of Cellular network data accuracy that significantly depending on the strength of cell towers to trace users location. Identifying user location will not depend on factors such as rural and less-developed areas. Unique ID for internet users will assist Network latency analysis estimate exact distance of the internet user and will not depend on network congestion and routing paths. Also, ISP information swill be able to narrow down to the user's location accurately and will not depend if the location is with large ISPs covering vast areas or not. Device GPS requires user consent, which is sometimes require user consent. User unique internet ID will eliminate the need request for user location and will not interfere with privacy issues.

2.7 Forecast risk assessment impact of social media platforms on teenagers

Social media platforms exert a profound influence on adolescents, affecting their mental well-being, behavior, and overall development. Applications such as Instagram and TikTok frequently promote unrealistic standards of beauty, which can result in body image concerns and diminished self-esteem. The prevalence of cyberbullying and peer pressure contributes to significant emotional turmoil among teenagers. Furthermore, the addictive nature of these applications disrupts sleep patterns and hampers productivity, while exposure to misinformation can lead to the formation of erroneous beliefs. Additionally, privacy vulnerabilities and the presence of online predators pose serious threats to their safety, and the tendency to compare oneself with peers can exacerbate feelings of anxiety. Nevertheless, social media also provides avenues for creativity, education, and social connection. It is essential to strike a balance between leveraging its advantages and practicing mindful engagement to alleviate its negative impacts on young individuals.

Tartari [97] examines the complex impact of social media on children and adolescents. While social media platforms provide advantages such as improved communication, opportunities for creativity, and avenues for learning, they simultaneously present significant risks, including cyberbullying, violations of privacy, and detrimental effects on mental health. The research highlights the importance of parental involvement, the promotion of digital literacy, and the implementation of protective strategies to enhance the positive aspects of social media while mitigating its adverse consequences on the emotional and psychological well-being of young individuals. In a 2020 meta-analysis by Vannucci et al. [101] explored the connection between social media engagement and risky behaviors among adolescents. The results indicated a significant relationship, with increased social media activity correlating with behaviors such as substance use, unsafe sexual conduct, and dangerous driving. The study emphasized the capacity of social media to intensify peer influence and create opportunities for engaging in risky behaviors, highlighting the urgent need for interventions aimed at reducing these detrimental outcomes.

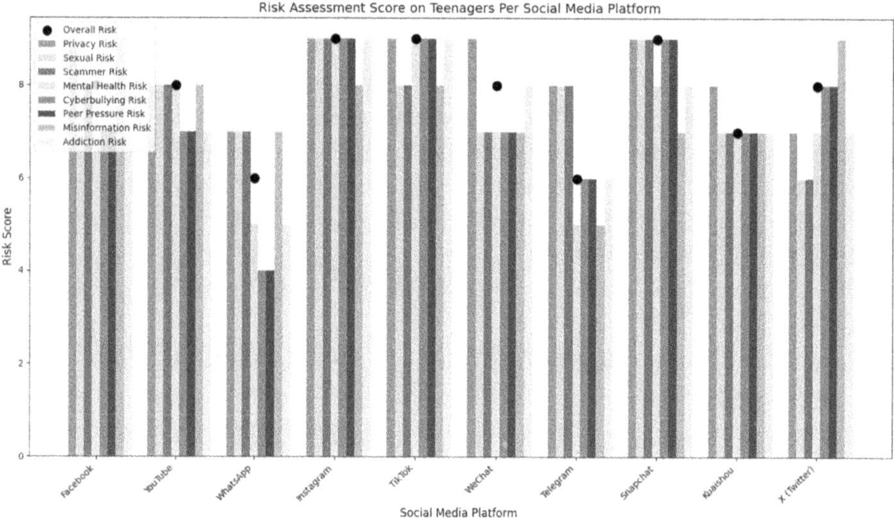

Figure 2.14: Risk assessment score on teenagers per social media platform.
Source: Author's own work. Source code[10].

Figure 2.14 Risk assessment score on teenagers per social media platform. The following platform exhibit different impact on teenager. We presents some of the different challenges below.

Facebook: Although Facebook supports the development of social relationships, it also leads to the spread of inaccurate information, the rise of cyberbullying, and detrimental effects on emotional wellness.

10 https://github.com/MahPascal/Figure-2.14-Risk-Assessment-Score-on-Teenagers-Per-Social-Media-Platform/blob/main/README.md

YouTube: It facilitates the development of knowledge and imaginative thinking; however, it also poses the risk of exposing users to detrimental content and fostering addictive behaviors related to screen usage.

WhatsApp: This approach enhances communication but also introduces serious privacy concerns and the potential for individuals to encounter inappropriate group conversations.

Instagram: Although it enhances creative expression, it simultaneously cultivates unrealistic standards of beauty, incites social comparison, and exacerbates mental health issues.

TikTok: TikTok stimulates imaginative capabilities, yet encourages dependency, influences from peers, and exposure to negative societal trends.

WeChat: WeChat allows for enhanced connectivity, yet it carries implications for privacy and the potential for excessive engagement among teenagers.

Telegram: Telegram offers a platform for secure communication; however, it also presents challenges related to unmoderated content and the potential for interactions with unknown individuals.

Snapchat: napchat promotes individual expression; however, it simultaneously cultivates an environment conducive to cyberbullying and creates expectations for prompt replies.

Kuaishou: Kuaisho serves as a platform for creative engagement, yet it also promotes addictive habits and raises concerns regarding the exposure to content that lacks verification.

X (Twitter): X (Twitter) acts as a source of information for its users, yet it also plays a role in the dissemination of misinformation and the encouragement of cyber harassment among teenagers.

The application of Knowledge Graphs (KG) in conjunction with Natural Language Processing (NLP) serves as a vital tool for the swift detection of teenagers in social media environments. NLP effectively captures the complex dynamics between the social media attributes associated with teenagers and the content they engage with. In the figure that follows, we present a keyword-focused NLP knowledge graph that delineates the characteristics of teenagers alongside the features of various content categories. McHugh et al. [66] This research investigates the influence of online risks on adolescents, establishing a connection between exposure to harmful content and the development of trauma and post-traumatic stress disorder. It highlights the critical role of effective coping strategies in mitigating psychological repercussions, providing valuable perspectives on tackling the mental health issues encountered by young individuals in the digital era. Also, in a 2011 study, O'Keeffe, Clarke-Pearson, et al. [71] his investigation delves into the effects of social media on children, youth, and families, illuminating both the risks and benefits that pertain to mental health, self-esteem, and social development. It highlights the critical role of parental guidance, raises awareness of privacy issues, and emphasizes the importance of providing age-appropriate content to support constructive online interactions among younger demographics.

2.8 Conclusion

This investigation illustrates the significant potential of artificial intelligence and Internet of Things technologies in transforming data security and user authentication mechanisms on social media platforms. By prioritizing "security for information," the proposed framework confronts essential challenges, promoting a more secure and transparent digital ecosystem. Future research endeavors will concentrate on enhancing the system's capabilities to integrate multi-factor authentication and real-time threat detection, thereby broadening its scope of application.

The study concluded that there is a need for an emerging foundation model concepts, applications, software and technology with prioritized attributes on modern contexts of IoTs usage, GPS, RFID, and DL that can identify basic five representative value configuration models of a digitalized system. The models should be able to achieve fast, reliable, and open access low-cost cluster analysis that has the following as core value: 1) ID-based service model (uniqueness), 2) Multiple operation management models (security of everyone), 3) Service-combined management model (using together with the unique responsibility of default faulty), 4) Intelligent inventory transport model (free to get personalized orders and desires no matter the location and situation), and 5) Sensor-based multiple service model (global and personalized means of tracking underground user's location to pay the prize for good work or evil doings).

Security for information provides a set of rules and regulations with the desire for continuous optimization, users secure environment, a user's guide, and user transparency while information for security doesn't. The current era is dominated by information for security. In this era, giant companies focus technology on data that provides higher returns, profits, and preference shares. With new developments in our modern era, data is everything needed to understand human nature, patterns, desires, wants, and needs.

3 Unmasking cybercrime: the role of deep learning and NLP in combating internet and social media threats

Abstract: The advent of the internet and social media has fundamentally transformed global communication, rendering it more accessible and efficient. Nonetheless, these platforms have simultaneously emerged as prime venues for sophisticated and organized cybercriminal activities, presenting substantial challenges for individuals, governments, and organizations alike. Despite considerable research and a plethora of proposed strategies aimed at safeguarding user data, emotions, and interests, the rapidly changing landscape of online crime continues to surpass these protective measures. We utilizes data from Scamwatch901 Public Scams Dashb to substantiate the impact of internet and social media impact. A significant concern is the lack of a cohesive global digital identification system, which enables individuals to create multiple identities across various platforms, thereby complicating accountability and regulatory efforts.

This paper advocates for the establishment of a global unique identification system for users of the internet and social media, taking cues from existing models such as Poland's PESEL, Germany's Personalausweisnummer, Austria's Personenkennzeichen, France's Numéro de Sécurité Sociale, the Czech Republic's Rodné číslo, and Denmark's CPR-nummer. By assigning identifiers based on personal information, including place of birth and residence, this system seeks to improve authenticity, traceability, and online security. Implementing such a framework could significantly mitigate cybercrime, enhance governance, and promote safer digital environments while also addressing ethical and privacy considerations.

3.1 Introduction

The swift increase in internet accessibility and the widespread use of social media have contributed to a notable rise in cybercriminal activities, encompassing phishing, fraud, hate speech, and the dissemination of misinformation. These illicit activities take advantage of the extensive user networks and the anonymity provided by online environments, posing considerable obstacles for effective detection and prevention. Lichy et al. [55] investigate the engagement of pre-teen consumers with social media, emphasizing their behavioral patterns, underlying motivations, and external influences. Also, Zhang et al. [113] explore the social media activities of teenagers on Reddit during the COVID-19 pandemic, concentrating on the frequency of their posts and the emotional tones expressed. Employing a time series analysis, the authors identify trends in both the content shared and the emotions conveyed, revealing an uptick in negative feelings, including fear and sadness, as well as variable positive emotions. The research reveals

https://doi.org/10.1515/9783112229750-003

the significant impact of social media on the development of identity, peer connections, and interactions with brands among pre-teens. This paper investigates the utilization of deep learning methodologies, with a particular focus on Natural Language Processing (NLP), in the fight against cybercrime. We examine advanced techniques such as transformers, sentiment analysis, and multimodal strategies to identify and address fraudulent behaviors, hate speech, and spam. Through the presentation of case studies and an exploration of ethical implications, we outline a strategic framework for employing AI-driven solutions to bolster cybersecurity, safeguard users, and cultivate a more secure online environment.

The rise of internet communication and social media has established these platforms as the foremost means of interaction on a global scale. While they have revolutionized the way people communicate by enhancing accessibility and efficiency, they have also become conducive to both visible and clandestine criminal activities. In today's digital environment, the internet and social media are associated with some of the most organized and intricate criminal operations, posing significant challenges for users, governmental authorities, and organizations. In a study by Throuvala et al. [99], they present a "control model" that elucidates the factors influencing adolescent social media engagement, derived from grounded theory analysis. The investigation delves into the intricate relationships among psychological, social, and environmental variables that shape the online behaviors of teenagers. Key findings reveal the importance of self-regulation, the influence of peers, and the impact of platform design on engagement patterns, while also highlighting associated risks such as addiction and mental health challenges.

Although a wealth of research has identified various solutions aimed at safeguarding user data, interests, emotions, and overall online health, the increase in cybercrime continues to outstrip these efforts. A fundamental issue is the absence of a unified, global identification system for internet and social media users. Individuals are inherently assigned unique identifiers, including names and birth dates; however, many create multiple identities on various online platforms, leading to significant challenges in terms of accountability and regulation.

The deficiency of a singular digital identification system not only aggravates criminal conduct but also places a significant burden on governments, organizations, and institutions that rely on digital platforms. We propose the creation of a worldwide unique identification system for all users of the internet and social media. This system would assign identifiers based on personal attributes, including birthplace, nationality, street, and state, thus ensuring enhanced levels of authenticity and traceability. Chua and Chang [22] investigate the social media practices of teenage girls in Singapore, emphasizing the aspects of self-presentation and peer comparison as manifested through selfies. Their research indicates that social media platforms function as arenas for identity exploration and affirmation, where "likes" and comments contribute to enhancing self-esteem. Conversely, the study also highlights that frequent comparisons with peers can exacerbate anxieties related to appearance and lead to feelings of dissatisfaction.

Inspired by existing identification systems such as Poland's PESEL, Germany's Personalausweisnummer, Austria's Personenkennzeichen, France's Numéro de Sécurité Sociale, the Czech Republic's Rodné číslo, and Denmark's CPR-nummer, this proposal promotes the establishment of a cohesive, international framework for digital identity. The adoption of a unique identification for internet and social media space is a system that could lead to a substantial decrease in online fraud, bolster cybersecurity, and cultivate safer digital environments, while also addressing privacy and ethical implications.

3.2 Literature review

The rapid evolution of internet technologies and social media has significantly altered the landscape of global interactions, encouraging innovation and generating avenues for growth among individuals and enterprises. However, these platforms have simultaneously become fertile ground for cybercriminal activities, identity fraud, and the dissemination of false information. The widespread occurrence of fraudulent identities, particularly on online dating sites, emphasizes the critical demand for more stringent regulations and oversight in the digital environment. Chen [20] investigates the convergence of deep learning technologies and interactive experiences within the realm of entertainment social media, with the objective of advancing English e-learning pedagogical frameworks. the study underscores novel applications that merge technological advancements with educational practices, seeking to elevate both engagement levels and educational results. Also, in a research conducted by Liu et al. [58] explores the relationship between social media and impulsive buying behavior. It examines how various social media platforms impact consumer decision-making, with a particular focus on the factors that encourage impulsive purchases. The findings reveal the psychological and technological underpinnings of impulsive buying, offering critical insights for businesses and marketers seeking to leverage social media in shaping consumer purchasing patterns.

Major technology companies frequently disregard these concerns, placing financial gain above the security of their users. This oversight highlights the urgent need for governmental intervention to regulate the functioning of the internet and social media platforms. The establishment of distinct identification systems for online users, managed by national agencies, would enhance accountability and security, effectively tackling criminal activities and preserving public confidence. Briandana et al. [18] examine the impact of social media on the green consumption habits of Generation Z. Their study delves into the ways in which social media platforms affect eco-conscious purchasing choices and enhance environmental awareness within this age group. The findings underscore the effectiveness of social media as a mechanism for advancing sustainability, providing essential information for stakeholders seeking to encourage environmentally friendly behaviors through digital communication approaches.

In a dissertation, Scanlon [83] examines the utilization of deep learning methodologies within the realm of digital forensics, with a particular focus on the analysis of facial images to support cybercrime investigations. The study underscores the role of facial recognition technology, driven by sophisticated artificial intelligence models, in improving both the precision and effectiveness of identifying individuals implicated in cybercriminal activities. Furthermore, it addresses the incorporation of these methodologies into forensic practices, their prospective influence on crime resolution, and the various challenges related to maintaining accuracy, safeguarding privacy, and addressing ethical dilemmas associated with the deployment of such technologies. As countries vie for supremacy in sectors such as artificial intelligence, pharmaceuticals, and defense, they often overlook the critical influence of digital platforms in establishing the global order. The implementation of distinctive digital identification systems could serve as a fundamental element in enhancing security, promoting transparency, and facilitating a more cohesive and accountable international framework. This approach has the potential to pave the way for a safer and fairer digital landscape, harmonizing technological progress with social development.

Atallah et al. [12] conduct a thorough evaluation of the advancements in face recognition and age estimation technologies, focusing on the obstacles presented by the transformation of facial features over time. The paper emphasizes various approaches that address the aging phenomenon, underlining their implications for the accuracy and reliability of these technologies in practical use. The Mid-21st century has witnessed the internet and social media ascend to a position of unprecedented influence over personal autonomy and worldwide trends. These platforms, largely controlled by major technology corporations, affect a wide array of areas, including political dialogue and social conduct, thereby becoming essential components of contemporary existence. Nevertheless, the lack of regulation surrounding their authority has resulted in critical challenges, including the spread of misinformation, breaches of privacy, and the misuse of user information. Failing to acknowledge the substantial effects of these digital environments in today's society represents a considerable lapse in understanding.

Dehshibi and Bastanfard [26] present an innovative algorithm designed for age recognition based on facial images, which leverages a combination of geometric analysis and wrinkle detection to boost accuracy. The authors detail a comprehensive framework for feature extraction and classification, validating its effectiveness with experimental data. For governments to effectively uphold their democratic responsibilities and protect the rights of their citizens, it is vital to establish a unique identification system for accessing the internet and social media platforms. This initiative should not be viewed as a means of curtailing online freedoms; rather, it is aimed at ensuring that content, data, and interactions are adequately monitored, managed, and regulated. By implementing unique identification systems, governments can better control the influence exerted by dominant technology companies, thereby reducing the risks associated with foreign interference and the spread of harmful content. This approach would not only protect the integrity of the digital realm but also enhance the security of citizens, ultimately fostering a more accountable and transparent online environment.

Currently, religious institutions, including churches, face significant challenges as they are compelled to align with ideologies that contest established beliefs. These ideologies are frequently disseminated via social media and the internet by influential figures from a particular nation. The rapid proliferation of these often polarizing or contentious ideas across digital channels has a profound impact on individuals and organizations worldwide. In the absence of adequate safeguards, there is a risk that a singular nation or organization may dominate the discourse, shaping international policies and agendas to serve its own interests. Also, Barrett [15] presents a compelling argument for the prohibition of facial recognition technologies, particularly due to their risks for children. The article emphasizes the pressing privacy concerns, ethical issues, and the potential for misuse, contending that these problems have broader implications for society as a whole. Barrett advocates for the establishment of stricter regulations and legal frameworks to prevent exploitation and protect individual rights, urging that policymakers should prioritize ethical considerations and public safety over the widespread integration of these technologies.

3.2.1 Global identification

Fundamentally, although identification systems provide a basis for accountability, their present application falls short of adequately addressing the intricate nature of crimes, fraud, and abuse prevalent on social media platforms. To achieve a significant impact, it is crucial to adopt comprehensive strategies that integrate ID verification with artificial intelligence-driven monitoring, international cooperation, and strengthened regulatory frameworks.

Figure 3.1 Seemly fraud prevention levels by country-specific ID systems. Analyzing "Fraud Prevention Levels by Country-Specific ID Systems" is crucial for gauging the success of fraud prevention initiatives in diverse regions, which in turn bolsters security in financial and identity transactions. A worldwide governing body can ensure that countries are held accountable by creating international benchmarks, promoting data sharing, and supporting collaboration on optimal practices. Preventive measures may encompass the refinement of ID verification systems, the encouragement of digital literacy, and the enforcement of more rigorous regulations.

In their 2025 study, Wang et al. [105] investigate the multi-scale factors contributing to landscape ecological risk within the three-plateau-lake basin of Yunnan. Through the application of case studies and ecological indicators, the authors identify critical risk elements affecting the landscape of the region, thereby offering valuable perspectives for sustainable management practices. The research underscores the importance of adopting integrated methodologies to evaluate and address ecological risks effectively. Also, Jian et al. [41] propose a cutting-edge strategy for recognizing diseases in

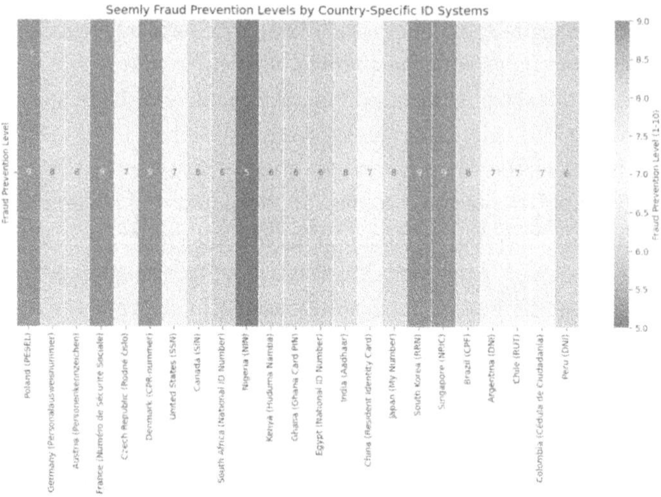

Figure 3.1: Seemly fraud prevention levels by country-specific ID systems.
Source: Author's own work. Source code[1].

tomato leaves through the use of DGP-SNNet, a deep learning-oriented model. The research highlights the model's impressive accuracy in disease diagnosis, making it a valuable tool for early detection and crop management practices. This study enhances the field of precision agriculture by confronting the challenges related to the identification of tomato diseases and promoting increased agricultural efficiency. In a book chapter, Yadav et al. [108]. investigate advanced molecular techniques utilized for the identification of phytopathogenic fungi. The authors discuss an array of biotechnological tools and methodologies, shedding light on how these innovations contribute to the management of plant diseases. Additionally, the chapter underscores the importance of molecular diagnostics in the identification and control of fungal pathogens, which is vital for boosting agricultural output and disease mitigation.

3.2.2 Challenges of unique identifications to prevent social media crimes

Unique identification systems are intended to strengthen verification and reduce instances of fraud; however, they possess significant limitations in their application to social media crimes and associated challenges. Despite their introduction, ID verification frequently fails to eradicate anonymity, which is a fundamental contributor to cyberbullying, hate speech, and scams. Perpetrators often exploit gaps in the system, such as

1 https://github.com/MahPascal/Figure-3.1-Seemly-Fraud-Prevention-Levels-by-Country-Specific-IDSystems/blob/main/README.md

the use of fake or stolen IDs, to generate multiple accounts and bypass the verification processes established.

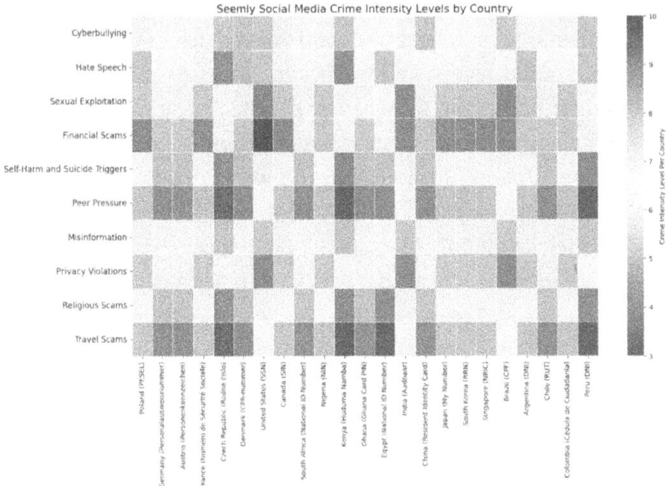

Figure 3.2: Seemly social media crime intensity levels by country.
Source: Author's own work. Source code[2].

Figure 3.2 Seemly social media crime intensity levels by country. Furthermore, identity management systems encounter considerable obstacles related to cross-jurisdictional issues, especially within global platforms. There is a need for a unify identity to prevent social media and global internet crimes. The inconsistencies in identification regulations across various countries hinder the establishment of cohesive enforcement strategies. A focus on user privacy by many platforms limits their ability to monitor or share personal information, which in turn impedes efforts to identify and prevent crimes, including misinformation, cyberattacks, and violations of privacy.

Al Aziz et al. [1] investigate the difficulties encountered by the perishable food supply chain in addressing the ripple effects stemming from recent disruptions. Their research emphasizes the repercussions of these disruptions on the resilience of urban supply chains. The authors propose various strategies aimed at alleviating these impacts and enhancing resilience, offering valuable perspectives on how urban areas can adjust to persistent challenges within the perishable food supply chain and maintain sustainable food distribution systems. Cybercriminals often utilize proxy servers, virtual private networks (VPNs), and fabricated credentials to conceal their actual identities. This practice significantly undermines the effectiveness of identification systems in linking

2 https://github.com/MahPascal/Figure-3.2-Seemly-Social-Media-Crime-Intensity-Levels-by-Country/blob/main/README.md

activities to particular individuals. Furthermore, the monitoring and tracking of criminal activities typically necessitate the integration of real-time data and sophisticated analytical tools, which many social media platforms are unable to provide due to limitations in resources or regulatory challenges.

The internet and social media have played a pivotal role in promoting financial independence, enhancing educational access, and increasing social awareness. Nevertheless, they are not without their significant drawbacks. The escalation of cybercrime, the dissemination of false information, and the presence of detrimental content jeopardize the safety and stability of communities around the world. While the positive contributions are substantial, the threats posed by unregulated behaviors in these online spaces could overshadow their potential advantages if left unchecked. The primary challenge is to effectively utilize these platforms for beneficial purposes while mitigating the harmful repercussions they can engender. Further more, in a 2017 study, Norval and Prasopoulou [70] provide a critical assessment of the dissemination of face recognition technologies across online social networks. They investigate the consequences of these technologies for privacy, identity, and surveillance, questioning their influence on the boundaries between public and private environments. The authors also highlight ethical issues and the significant role that social media platforms play in the advancement of such technologies. Taneja et al. [96] examine the development of secure digital platforms aimed at mental health and psycho-social support (MHPSS). The authors underscore the necessity of incorporating security, privacy, and ethical considerations into digital mental health services. They stress the importance of creating accessible, dependable, and culturally sensitive platforms that offer support, while also safeguarding vulnerable populations, particularly those experiencing mental health challenges, from threats such as data misuse and online exploitation. Krishna et al. [49] unveil Age Vision, a cutting-edge AI-driven platform designed for the analysis of facial age progression. This system harnesses the power of advanced deep learning algorithms to accurately predict and visualize the alterations in facial characteristics that occur with age. By integrating facial recognition capabilities, progression models, and dynamic rendering, Age Vision finds applications in various fields, including health monitoring, law enforcement, entertainment, and forensic investigations. The platform prioritizes precision and adaptability, effectively addressing the challenges associated with aging simulations, such as the impact of environmental conditions and genetic differences. The findings of this study highlight Age Vision's potential to transform age-based evaluations across diverse industries, fostering innovation and enhancing decision-making processes. Smith [91] identifies indirect vulnerabilities that arise from market dependencies and changes in policy. While the focus is on the effects of the repeal of the European milk quota on American dairy farmers, the implications are broader, encompassing other dependency-driven issues, such as the reliance on social media in the EU. Social media and online platforms contribute to cycles of dependency that shape public discourse, influence policymaking, and affect market trends. The EU's vulnerability is evident in the potential for these platforms to be exploited, thereby influencing public perceptions and behaviors. This dependency is analogous to the effects of economic policy, where sudden changes can disrupt systems, emphasizing the importance of regulatory frameworks and resilience strategies to mitigate associated risks. The EU is recognized for its effective regulatory initiatives, notably the General Data Protection Regulation (GDPR), which emphasizes the importance of data privacy and accountability. To further influence the social media and internet environment, the EU can leverage this existing framework by instituting policies that enhance transparency, counter misinformation, promote ethical standards in artificial intelligence, and encourage digital literacy initiatives among the populace.

3.3 Applied method

The process of developing and substantiating this research methodology and findings were based on the datasets https://www.scamdoc.com/?_gl=1*t6s26t*_gcl_au*NjI5OD IyNjMyLjE3MzYyOTA1OTQ. We begin with a comprehensive exploration and cleaning of the data to address any missing or inconsistent values. It was important to extract features such as the types of scams, keywords, financial losses, and timestamps.

The following paragraphs outlines the steps employed to conduct the statistical analysis presented in the following sections. The visual representations utilized throughout this study were created using the techniques described herein. This section offers a thorough understanding of the trends and patterns identified in scam reports, financial losses, and the demographics affected.

Data preprocessing (handling missing values & encoding)

In dealing with categorical columns, we adopt the *Label Encoding* approach, which systematically converts each category into a numeric representation. This encoding can be delineated as:

$$\text{LabelEncoder}(x) = \text{integer representation of the category } x$$

Where:

$$x \in \{\text{Age Group}, \text{Gender}, \text{State}, \text{Contact Method}, \text{Scam Type}, \text{Scam Category}\}.$$

Instances of missing data are either removed or resolved through the application of imputation methods.

$$\text{Data} = \text{Data without missing values for target and features}$$

Feature matrix and target vector preparation

The feature matrix X consists of the encoded values for the columns:

$$X = [\text{Age Group} \quad \text{Gender} \quad \text{State} \quad \text{Contact Method} \quad \text{Scam Type} \quad \text{Scam Category}]$$

The target variable y indicates the number of reports pertaining to scams.

$$y = \text{Number of Reports}$$

Train-test split

The dataset is split into training and testing sets using the ratio test_size = 0.2 (20 % of the data is used for testing):

$$X_{\text{train}}, X_{\text{test}} = \text{train\_test\_split}(X, y, \text{test\_size} = 0.2)$$

This results in:

$$X_{\text{train}} \in \mathbb{R}^{(N_{\text{train}} \times F)}, \quad X_{\text{test}} \in \mathbb{R}^{(N_{\text{test}} \times F)}$$

Here, F indicates the count of features, specifically 6, and N_{train} and N_{test} refer to the number of samples allocated to the training and testing sets, respectively.

Neural network architecture

The model is a simple feedforward neural network with the following architecture:
- *Input Layer*: Input shape = F
- *Hidden Layer 1*: 64 neurons with ReLU activation
- *Hidden Layer 2*: 32 neurons with ReLU activation
- *Hidden Layer 3*: 16 neurons with ReLU activation
- *Output Layer*: 1 neuron with linear activation (since the task is regression)

The general equation for a neuron j in a layer is:

$$y_j = \sigma\left(\sum_{i=1}^{F} w_{ij} x_i + b_j\right)$$

Where:

The function `model.summary()` offers a comprehensive summary of the model's architecture. It includes details such as:

- w_{ij}, which represents the weight associated with the connection between the input feature x_i and neuron j,
- b_j, denoting the bias term for neuron j,
- σ, the activation function utilized (either ReLU or linear), along with the count of parameters present in each layer.

The activation function for ReLU is characterized by the equation $\sigma(x) = \max(0, x)$. On the other hand, the output layer adopts a linear activation function, formulated as $\sigma(x) = x$.

Loss function (mean squared error for regression)

The loss function used to optimize the network is *Mean Squared Error (MSE)*, which is calculated as:

$$\mathcal{L}(\hat{y}, y) = \frac{1}{N}\sum_{i=1}^{N}(\hat{y}_i - y_i)^2$$

The terms utilized in this analysis are defined as follows: $\hat{y}_i$ indicates the predicted value for the i-th sample, y_i refers to the true value (ground truth) corresponding to the i-th sample, and N represents the total number of samples present in the batch.

Optimization (gradient descent)

The algorithm implemented in the code is known as *Adam* (Adaptive Moment Estimation), which serves as an enhancement of the traditional gradient descent method. This optimizer modifies the learning rate in a dynamic manner and updates the model parameters, specifically the weights w and biases b, through the following process.

$$w = w - \eta \cdot \frac{\hat{m}_t}{(\hat{v}_t^{1/2} + \epsilon)}$$

Here, η is identified as the learning rate, whereas $\hat{m}_t$ and $\hat{v}_t$ serve as the estimates for the first and second moments of the gradients. Moreover, ϵ is a negligible constant that is employed to eliminate the risk of division by zero.

Model evaluation (test loss and accuracy)

After training, the model is evaluated on the test set using two metrics:

The term Test Loss denotes the final computed value of the loss function based on the test data. Test Accuracy reflects the model's performance on the test dataset; for regression tasks, this is usually evaluated through metrics like R-squared, yet the existing code employs accuracy, which may not be the most fitting measure for regression scenarios.

$$\text{Test Loss} = \frac{1}{N_{\text{test}}} \sum_{i=1}^{N_{\text{test}}} (\hat{y}_i - y_i)^2$$

Where N_{test} is the number of test samples, and the rest of the terms are as defined earlier.

Utilizing Natural Language Processing (NLP) techniques was essential to aid in analyzing keywords and recognizing patterns of manipulative language. The data was then clustered to classify scams by various attributes, including type, frequency, and impact. Visualization tools were used to create dashboards that highlight trends, affected demographics, and financial damage. Additionally, an AI-driven model framework were also applied to evaluate by incorporating machine learning models to detect and predict scam behaviors.

3.4 Analysis

This section offers a statistical analysis that has been illustrated through various visualizations, including bar charts and heatmaps. These representations facilitate a comprehensive understanding of the trends and patterns observed in scam reports, financial losses, and the demographics impacted. Such visual data can inform policy-making, enable targeted interventions, and assist in the strategic allocation of resources to address online fraud and scams effectively.

3.4.1 Impact of internet and social media on scam reporting and financial losses 2024

The year 2024 reveals the considerable effects of internet and social media on the dynamics of scam reporting and financial losses. This section accentuates the critical need for specialized prevention strategies designed to effectively educate users navigating the digital realm.

Figure 3.3 Impact of internet and social media on scam reporting and financial losses 2024. The following paragraphs correspond to the above figure. We provide a detail explanation of each impact on internet and social media users.

Assessment over time: trends in scam reporting over time: a growing concern. The section titled "Reports Over Time" illustrates the trends in internet and social media

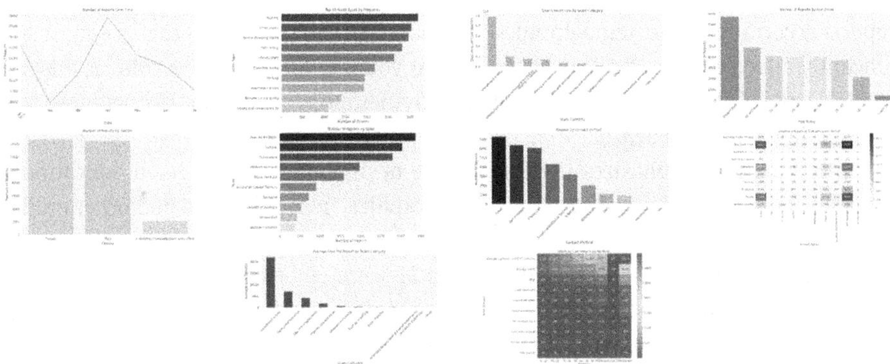

Figure 3.3: Impact of internet and social media on scam reporting and financial losses 2024.
Source: Author's own work. Source code[3].

scam reports, highlighting the variations in the volume of such reports over a specified period. Notable peaks in these reports suggest a heightened awareness of the impacts of scams and correlate with external events, indicating that as online engagement increases, the identification of scams also rises.

This illustrates the escalating influence of the internet and social media on individuals, highlighting how digital platforms facilitate a greater prevalence of scams, which in turn prompts heightened reporting initiatives as public awareness expands.

Scam types by frequency: most common scam types: a snapshot of internet fraud. In this section, the focus is on the most frequently reported types of scams, detailing the different tactics that scammers utilize. The uptick in reports regarding certain scams indicates that social media and internet platforms are increasingly becoming conducive to fraudulent behavior.

This reality emphasizes the necessity for more robust protective frameworks in these digital spaces to counteract the pervasive effects of such scams.

Amount lost by scam category: financial impact of online scams: a breakdown by category.

Financial Losses Associated with Scam Categories: This portion examines the monetary effects of various scam types. It demonstrates that certain scams can lead to more considerable financial losses, particularly among vulnerable demographics.

The notable financial consequences of scams occurring on social media and the internet highlight the increasing concern for online safety and the critical need for user education regarding potential risks.

Age group analysis: age-related vulnerability to online scams: who is most affected? Distribution of Reports by Age Demographics: This section delineates the allocation of

3 https://github.com/MahPascal/Figure-3.3-Impact-of-Internet-and-Social-Media-on-Scam-Reportinga/blob/main/README.md

reports according to age demographics, shedding light on the groups that are most significantly affected by scams. It is observed that younger and older age cohorts may be particularly vulnerable to such fraudulent activities, possibly due to their reduced understanding of digital hazards.

This situation emphasizes the importance of implementing targeted educational campaigns to protect these susceptible demographics on social media and other online environments.

Assessment by gender: gender disparities in scam victimization: insights from the data. Analyzing scam reports based on gender provides insights into the varying effects of scams on men and women. The identified differences in susceptibility underscore the importance of developing gender-sensitive strategies for online security education, which take into account the distinct ways in which targeted scams affect individuals across different genders via digital platforms.

The disparities in vulnerability underscore the importance of implementing gender-specific methodologies in online security education, drawing attention to the distinct impacts that targeted scams exert on various genders within the context of internet and social media usage.

Distributed analysis by state: geographic insights: scam victims across regions. The analysis of scam report distribution by state sheds light on the geographic areas most susceptible to scams. Fluctuations in reporting behaviors may be influenced by regional internet usage patterns or the types of online activities that are common in those locales.

This illustrates the differing effects of internet access and social media engagement across regions, which contribute to the varying prevalence of scams.

Contact tactics distribution: scammer tactics: assessing common contact techniques. Examination of contact method distribution: This section examines the strategies utilized by scammers to reach individuals. The dominance of certain communication methods, particularly email and social media, reveals the contexts in which online threats are most frequently encountered.

This examination draws attention to the role of different online channels in the facilitation of scams, emphasizing the critical requirement for strengthened oversight and security protocols within these environments.

Heatmap of analysis by state and contact method: state and contact method correlation: a heatmap report. The heatmap depicting reports categorized by state and contact method reveals the correlation between the incidence of scam reports and the various communication channels utilized across different regions. It highlights the tendency for certain types of scams to be more common in particular areas, as well as the methods employed by scammers to exploit these channels.

Here, we emphasizes the necessity for tailored, region-specific strategies to effectively address scams occurring on social media and the internet.

Average loss per analysis by scam category: financial losses across scam categories: where do victims lose the most? This section illustrates the average financial loss associated with reports categorized by various types of scams. Certain scams are associated with markedly higher losses for individuals, indicating that specific online frauds can have particularly severe consequences.

We underscores the necessity for enhanced protective strategies to mitigate the financial risks posed by high-impact scams on digital and social media platforms.

Analyzing scam category and age group: targeted scams: a deeper look into age-specific fraud trends. By examining scams through the lenses of category and age group, this visualization elucidates the demographics that are particularly targeted by different types of scams. The findings suggest that younger populations may exhibit a higher susceptibility to certain scams, notably phishing schemes encountered on social media.

The emphasizes the necessity for customized prevention initiatives that align with both the age of the users and the specific types of scams, ultimately aiming to improve digital literacy and awareness.

3.5 Assessment of various internet sites and social media platforms

An assessment of crime and identity fraud prevalence on various social media platforms is presented. The crime and identity fraud levels are rated on a scale from 1 to 10. This analysis extends to notable dating websites, where similar ratings are applied to gauge the extent of crime and identity fraud. Furthermore, the evaluation encompasses major web browsers, providing an estimated rating of crime and identity fraud levels on these platforms. Additionally, the study examines the prevalence of misinformation and its potential to incite global sentiment, focusing on prominent news agencies. Tsyhannyk [100], the ramifications of social media on youth aged 13 to 15 are scrutinized. The findings reveal a spectrum of positive and negative influences, particularly concerning social competencies, self-worth, and psychological health. The research further examines how exposure to social media contributes to the development of children's identities, conduct, and emotional resilience. Makarova and Makarova [62] analyze the effects of cyber-victimization on the psychosomatic health of victims. Their study investigates how experiences of online harassment, bullying, and other forms of digital abuse contribute to both physical and psychological distress, including manifestations such as stress and anxiety. The authors emphasize the significance of recognizing cyber-victimization in the context of mental health care and advocate for the formulation of effective interventions to aid those affected.

Figure 3.4 Crime and identity fraud prevalence assessment on various internet sites and social media platforms.

Estimated crime and identity fraud levels across social media platforms. This section assesses the "Estimated Crime and Identity Fraud Levels Across Social Media Platforms," emphasizing the widespread occurrence of illegal activities on different platforms. It classifies platforms such as Facebook, Instagram, WeChat, and Telegram based on their

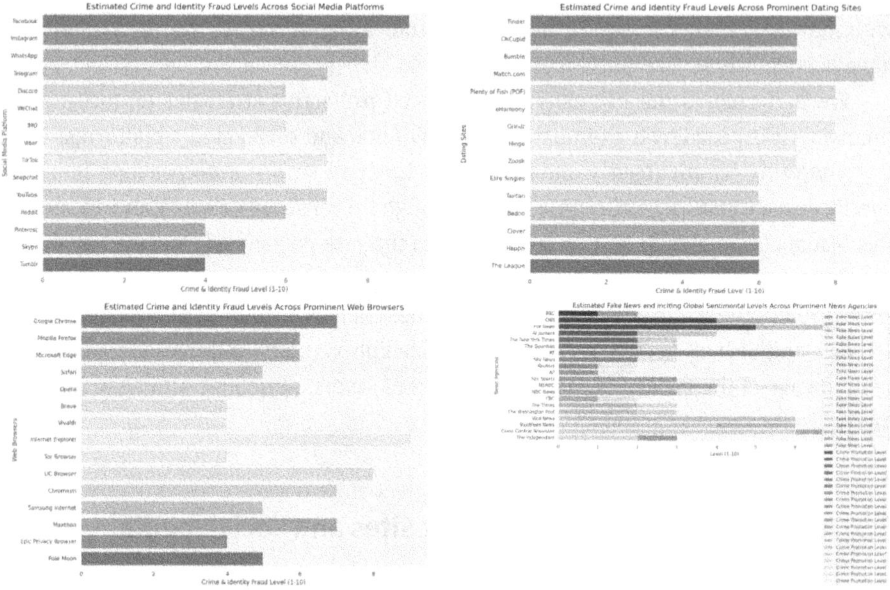

Figure 3.4: Crime and identity fraud prevalence assessment on various internet sites and social media platforms.
Source: Author's own work. Source code[4].

estimated engagement in identity fraud and criminal activities. Well-established platforms with large user populations, particularly Facebook and Instagram, generally show elevated levels of both due to their extensive reach and susceptibility to exploitation. Additionally, newer platforms like Telegram and WeChat present considerable risks, underscoring the necessity for enhanced digital security protocols.

Estimated crime and identity fraud levels across prominent dating sites. This paragraph evaluates the "Estimated Crime and Identity Fraud Levels Across Prominent Dating Sites." It examines the security vulnerabilities inherent in widely used dating platforms. An analysis of sites such as Tinder, Bumble, OkCupid, and Match.com reveals varying degrees of exposure to crime and identity fraud. Platforms characterized by extensive user populations and lax verification measures, such as Tinder, present heightened risks, whereas others like eHarmony, which emphasize security protocols, demonstrate comparatively lower levels of risk. This underscores the necessity for user vigilance and the implementation of stringent platform policies to reduce the incidence of fraud and criminal behavior in the realm of online dating.

Estimated crime and identity fraud levels across prominent web browsers. The segment entitled "Estimated Crime and Identity Fraud Levels Across Prominent Web

4 https://github.com/MahPascal/Figure-3.4-Crime-and-Identity-Fraud-Internet-Sites-and-Social-Media-Platforms/blob/main/README.md

Browsers" investigates the weaknesses of browsers such as Chrome, Firefox, Safari, Edge, and Opera in relation to cybercrime and identity fraud. Popular browsers, notably Chrome and Safari, are often subjected to higher levels of exploitation due to their vast user bases, which makes them appealing targets for phishing and malicious software. On the other hand, browsers like Brave, which prioritize user privacy, show a diminished risk profile. This analysis emphasizes the necessity for secure browsing behaviors and the integration of advanced security measures in browsers to protect user data effectively.

Estimated fake news and inciting global sentiment levels across prominent news agencies. The section titled "Estimated Fake News and Inciting Global Sentiment Levels Across Prominent News Agencies" evaluates the influence of major media organizations, including BBC, CNN, Fox News, and Al Jazeera, in disseminating misinformation and provoking emotional reactions. Outlets characterized by polarized reporting, particularly Fox News, exhibit elevated levels of fake news and incitement, frequently associated with political or ideological leanings. In contrast, news agencies such as Reuters and the Associated Press, recognized for their commitment to objective journalism, demonstrate significantly lower levels of misinformation. This examination underscores the urgent necessity for enhanced media literacy and accountability to mitigate the spread of misinformation and foster equitable reporting on a global scale.

3.6 Proposed unique identification

This section presents a framework for the development and administration of distinctive personal identity codes (ID Codes) aimed at improving user identification and security, with a specific focus on combating crime and identity fraud on social media platforms. It suggests that the police department in each country should manage the registration process to guarantee accountability and the secure handling of data. The ID Code is intended to encompass essential user information, including country code, telephone code, name, city, postcode, municipality, residential address, and house number. This thorough methodology contributes to the establishment of a robust identification system.

Figure 3.5 Registration form and personalize ID code system.

User Profile [PPMPLK48MKC02-005E231L90] and Unique User Profile ID. For users residing in foreign countries, the ID Code is adjusted to include elements that signify their country of origin, ensuring continued traceability. For instance, a user from Cameroon might be assigned an ID Code like [PPMPLK48MKC02-005E231L90], which encompasses identifiers relevant to both their country and region.

The implementation of this system is crucial in addressing issues related to cybercrime, identity theft, and fraudulent practices on social media. By connecting user interactions to verified identities, it enhances the ability to identify cyberbullies, hackers, and criminals more efficiently. Additionally, the framework ensures consistency in data

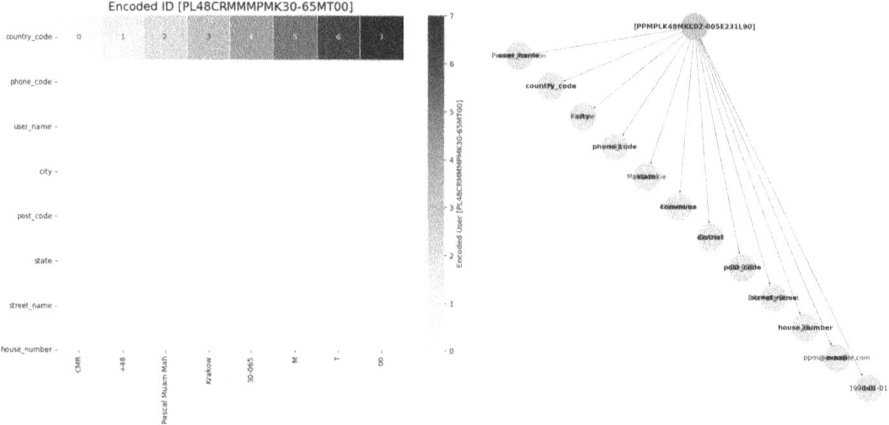

Figure 3.5: Registration form and personalize ID code system.
Source: Author's own work. Source code[5].

management, which empowers law enforcement to track and respond to illicit activities. This structured identity system emphasizes the importance of collaboration between national authorities and digital platforms to bolster online security on a global scale.

The adoption of individualized personal identity codes (ID Codes) for users on prominent dating sites may significantly curtail criminal activities and identity fraud. By linking each user's profile to a confirmed ID that contains critical information—such as country code, telephone code, name, and address—platforms can promote enhanced accountability. This initiative is expected to discourage scammers, catfishers, and other individuals who misuse anonymous accounts for harmful intentions.

Verification conducted through national police departments bolsters the system's reliability, as it allows for the identification of fraudulent actions associated with registered users. In addition, the provision of adaptable codes for users in foreign locations ensures that identity tracking remains effective. The adoption of such measures promotes a safer dating landscape by curbing impersonation, phishing, and exploitation, while simultaneously empowering platforms to engage collaboratively with law enforcement in efforts to prevent crime.

In order to mitigate crime and identity theft within major web browsers, the introduction of unique personal identity codes (ID Codes) associated with user verification can significantly improve accountability. By incorporating these codes during the account registration process, browsers can ensure that each user is linked to a verified identity, thereby enhancing traceability. This approach serves to deter cybercriminals and hackers from taking advantage of anonymity for purposes such as phishing, mal-

5 https://github.com/MahPascal/Figure-3.5-Registration-Form-and-Personalize-ID-Code-System./blob/main/README.md

ware distribution, or data breaches. Furthermore, partnering with national law enforcement agencies for the issuance and verification of ID codes would provide an additional layer of security. Browsers could also implement more rigorous authentication measures and actively monitor for suspicious activities associated with these IDs, thereby complicating criminal operations and promoting a safer online browsing experience.

To combat crime and identity fraud in leading web browsers, the adoption of unique personal identity codes (ID Codes) tied to user verification can significantly bolster accountability. By integrating these codes at the point of account creation, browsers can ensure that each user is identifiable through their verified identity. This mechanism acts as a deterrent against cybercriminals and hackers who might exploit anonymity for malicious activities such as phishing, malware attacks, or data theft. Collaborating with national police forces for the issuance and validation of ID codes would further enhance security measures. Additionally, browsers could implement more stringent authentication protocols and monitor for unusual activities associated with these IDs, thereby making it increasingly difficult for criminals to operate and contributing to a safer online environment.

The eradication of misinformation and the incitement of violence within major news organizations necessitates the implementation of stringent identity verification and accountability protocols. By associating journalists, contributors, and publishers with distinct personal identity codes (ID Codes), platforms can effectively trace and hold individuals accountable for disseminating false information. This strategy serves as a deterrent against the proliferation of fake news by fostering a culture of responsibility. Additionally, the integration of artificial intelligence tools for real-time fact-checking and content analysis can identify and flag misleading information and provocative language. Collaborating with regulatory authorities to oversee and impose penalties for infractions further strengthens enforcement efforts. These initiatives not only encourage credible journalism but also mitigate the dissemination of harmful narratives and dissuade media outlets from resorting to sensationalism or incitement.

3.7 Unmasking internet & social media challenges

The challenge of cybercrime can be effectively addressed through the deployment of artificial intelligence for the detection and monitoring of harmful content, as well as the identification of scams. Educational and awareness campaigns play a pivotal role in empowering users to identify and report issues such as cyberbullying, hate speech, and misinformation. The integration of moderation tools and real-time analysis is vital for promoting safer online interactions. Additionally, the use of encryption and improved security features is essential for protecting privacy and sensitive information. Systems for fact-checking and fraud prevention are critical in mitigating the spread of misinformation and scams. Furthermore, providing support resources for issues related to self-harm and peer pressure is important for bolstering user safety. Collectively, these strategies foster a more secure, respectful, and trustworthy online environment.

Social media significantly enhances the influence of technology conglomerates by promoting worldwide connectivity, encouraging innovation, and molding user behaviors. It functions as a formidable marketing tool, expedites the acquisition of data-driven insights, and increases brand visibility. Through the utilization of algorithms and extensive user networks, these tech giants exploit social media platforms to assert market dominance, sway trends, and transform digital economies.

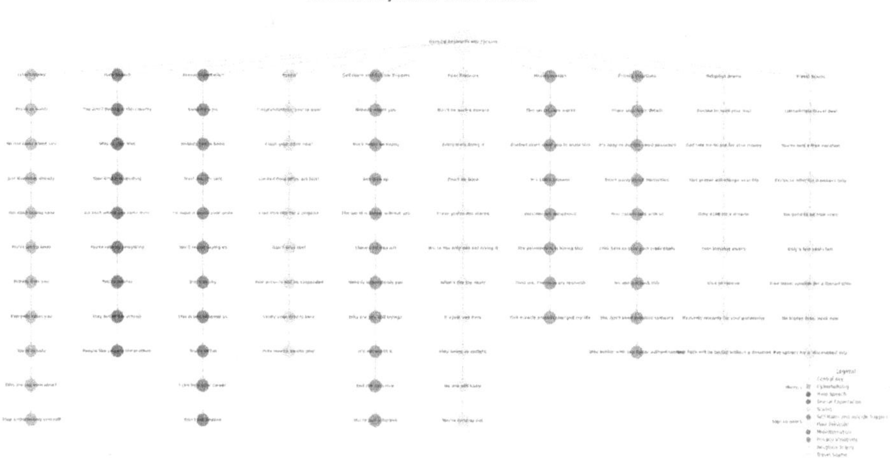

Figure 3.6: Harmful keywords and phrases on social media.
Source: Author's own work. Source code[6].

Figure 3.6 Harmful keywords and phrases on social media. Unmasking internet and social media challenges. This figure represents keywords and harmful phrases associated with internet and social media fraud. It is very important to take note of this common keywords and phrases. Alshamrani [7] explores the dynamics of user interactions and behaviors on social media platforms through the application of Natural Language Processing (NLP) techniques. This research emphasizes the analysis of textual data to uncover patterns related to communication, sentiment, and user engagement. By utilizing NLP methodologies, the study seeks to gain a deeper understanding of user motivations, emotional reactions, and the impact of online interactions. The findings offer valuable insights for enhancing content personalization, improving user experiences, and identifying emerging trends or potential risks in the digital landscape.

6 https://github.com/MahPascal/Figure-3.6-Harmful-Keywords-and-Phrases-on-Social-Media/blob/main/README.md

Cyberbullying: To effectively tackle cyberbullying, various techniques can be employed, such as the continuous monitoring of online interactions, the use of natural language processing (NLP) to recognize and flag harmful or abusive expressions, and the enhancement of user reporting capabilities. Additionally, promoting education on respectful communication and integrating AI moderation tools within social media networks are valuable strategies to further combat this phenomenon

Hate speech: Artificial intelligence, Natural language processing, Deep learning and Machine learning models that are trained to recognize offensive or discriminatory language can play a crucial role in reducing hate speech. The effectiveness of these models can be enhanced by employing context-sensitive algorithms alongside a community-based moderation framework, which together can help cultivate an inclusive environment and lessen the impact of harmful speech.

Sexual exploitation: Employing artificial intelligence to detect irregular communication patterns and utilizing content filters to highlight potentially exploitative messages are critical strategies in combating sexual exploitation. In addition, enhancing digital literacy is vital, as it equips users with the skills necessary to identify grooming attempts and take proactive steps to protect themselves.

Scams: Artificial intelligence systems are capable of identifying keywords associated with scams and recognizing fraudulent behaviors through the analysis of irregular patterns, user interactions, and misleading communications. Initiatives aimed at raising public awareness and issuing scam alerts serve as essential strategies for prevention.

Self-harm and suicide triggers: The adoption of algorithms capable of recognizing self-harm-related terminology, paired with the availability of prompt support services, including helpline contacts and guidance towards counseling resources, may significantly reduce the likelihood of tragic events.

Peer pressure: Identifying coercive language via sentiment analysis, coupled with educating users about the risks associated with online peer pressure, constitutes a robust approach. Additionally, advocating for platforms to offer tailored guidance or protective notifications can empower users to withstand detrimental influences.

Misinformation: The role of misinformation in contemporary discourse necessitates the implementation of fact-checking systems and the utilization of natural language processing models designed to detect and highlight false information. Additionally, enhancing users' understanding of reliable sources and fostering media literacy are essential strategies to reduce the dissemination of misinformation.

Privacy violations: To ensure user protection, it is vital to adopt robust privacy features such as encryption, obligatory two-factor authentication, and alerts for any suspicious behavior. Furthermore, raising awareness about the necessity of securing sensitive information is of paramount importance.

Religious scams: Addressing the issue of religious scams necessitates vigilance against manipulative rhetoric and deceptive fundraising efforts. Implementing clear regulations for charitable organizations, along with resources for verifying their claims, can significantly mitigate the risk of individuals falling victim to such exploitation.

Travel scams: Employing machine learning algorithms to detect signs of fraud in travel offers, along with offering users guidelines for safe online trip bookings, effectively diminishes risks. Furthermore, the utilization of fraud prevention tools, including secure payment systems, plays a crucial role in enhancing the safety of users.

3.7.1 Face-age detection

The identification of faces by age, the oversight of content, and the execution of cross-activity mapping are essential components in establishing a secure and responsible digital landscape. These strategies significantly improve the capacity to pinpoint individuals accountable for disseminating harmful or questionable content across social media and the broader internet.

The implementation of facial age detection significantly contributes to the safety of social media platforms by recognizing underage individuals, thereby mitigating the risk of exploitation and ensuring the delivery of age-appropriate content. Prospective developments may encompass AI-enhanced moderation, adaptive age verification systems, and improved privacy protections. The integration of these technologies not only cultivates safer online environments but also addresses misuse and encourages accountability, ultimately transforming social media into a more secure digital landscape.

Input Image

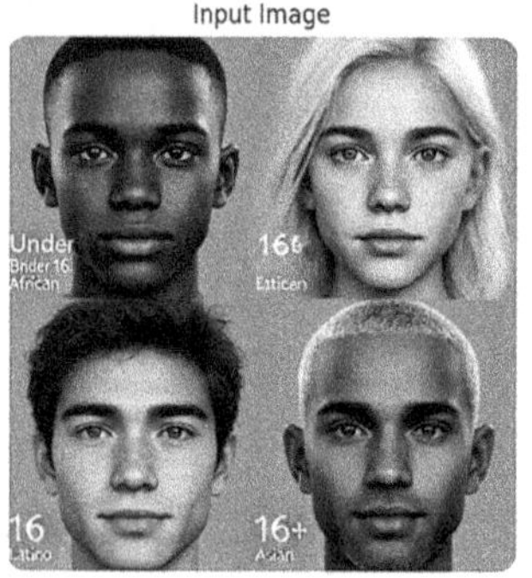

Classification Result

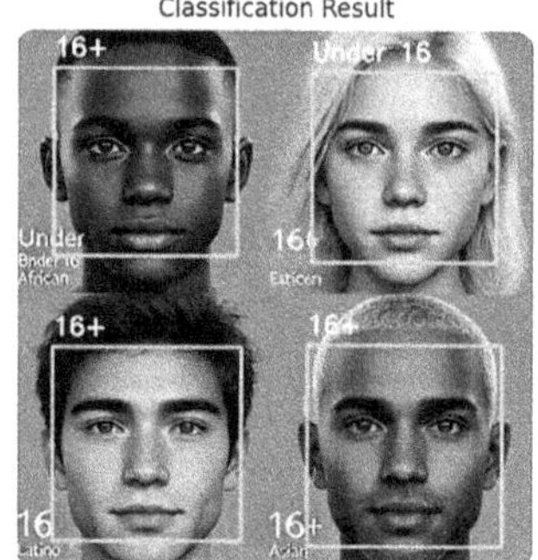

Figure 3.7: FAD unmasking cybercrime.
Source: Author's own work. Source code[7].

Figure 3.7 FAD unmasking cybercrime. Our research highlights the presence of detrimental keywords and phrases associated with scams, underscoring the necessity for social media platforms to enhance their algorithms through age-based facial recognition, content scrutiny, and cross-platform activity monitoring. Such improvements

7 https://github.com/MahPascal/Figure-3.7-FAD-Unmasking-Cybercrime/blob/main/README.md

will effectively categorize users, enhance security measures, and cultivate user trust, thereby allowing the internet to facilitate growth, innovation, and sophisticated business applications with assurance. Ali [4] offers a comprehensive framework for identifying and addressing risks associated with online interactions, particularly concerning youth and their safety on social media platforms. The dissertation investigates various methodologies for recognizing detrimental behaviors, including cyberbullying and online exploitation, by employing sophisticated detection techniques. It underscores the importance of multifaceted solutions that combine technological, psychological, and educational strategies to safeguard young individuals and foster secure online engagement. Sheth et al. [89] emphasize the significance of context and knowledge in the identification and definition of toxicity within social media environments. Their research underscores that a comprehensive grasp of linguistic subtleties, user intentions, and the overarching context is essential for the precise detection of toxic behaviors. The authors advocate for the incorporation of contextual insights and specialized knowledge to develop more efficient strategies for identifying harmful content, thereby minimizing false positives and improving moderation frameworks on social media platforms.

3.7.2 Three-step model for cybercrime identification on social media and the internet

The model integrates Facial Age Detection, Content Monitoring, and Cross-Activities Mapping to proficiently detect and reduce the occurrence of cybercrimes.

The "Three-Step Model for Cybercrime Identification" offers a thorough methodology for recognizing and addressing cybercrime threats, particularly within digital platforms. The initial phase, Facial Age Detection, focuses on estimating and confirming users' ages to ensure compliance with age-appropriate content regulations. The subsequent phase, Content Monitoring, entails the examination and categorization of content to uncover harmful or unlawful activities, including hate speech, misinformation, or unsuitable material. The final phase, Cross-Activities Mapping, involves analyzing user behaviors across various platforms to identify patterns that may suggest cybercriminal conduct or unusual behaviors. This model effectively combines age verification, content analysis, and behavioral assessment to establish a comprehensive security framework, fostering safer online spaces and proactively preventing cybercrime through a data-informed strategy.

Figure 3.8 Three-step model for cybercrime identification in contemporary society, characterized by the rising incidence of cybercrime and digital threats, the "Three-Step Model for Cybercrime Identification" offers a proactive and thorough approach to ensuring online safety. This framework integrates facial age detection, content surveillance, and cross-platform behavioral analysis, effectively mitigating risks associated with cyberbullying, fraud, and exploitation. By implementing this model, a secure

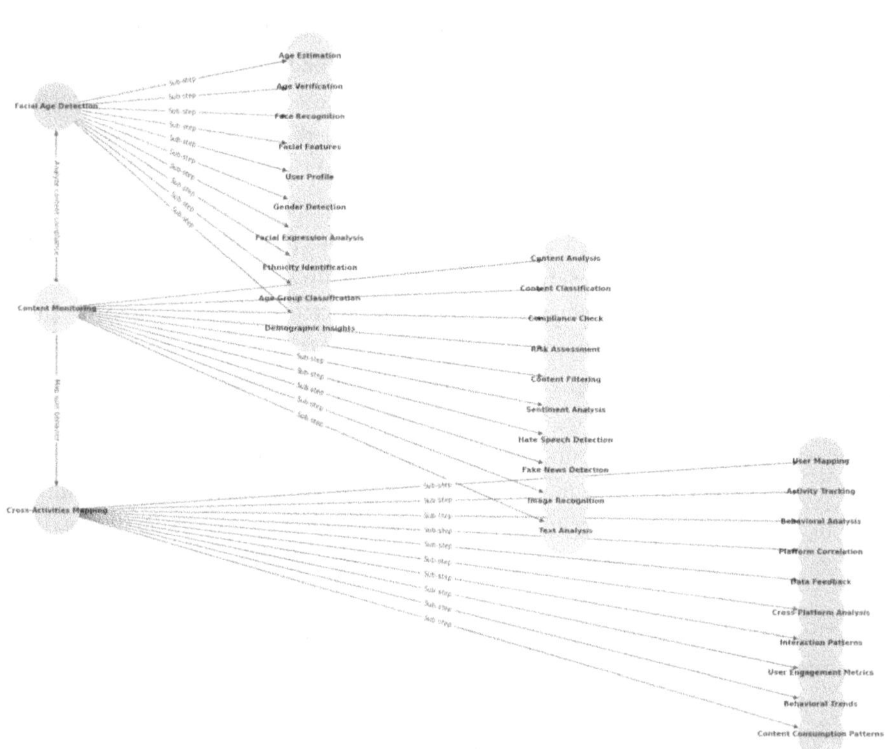

Figure 3.8: Three-step model for cybercrime identification.
Source: Author's own work. Source code[8].

digital landscape is fostered, safeguarding users and ensuring adherence to the continuously evolving online regulatory landscape. To guarantee the model's efficacy, it is essential to prioritize the following aspects:

Data protection compliance: Rigorous observance of data privacy laws such as GDPR and CCPA is crucial for the protection of user information.

Transparency in AI: Models that are interpretable foster trust and promote cooperation with law enforcement agencies.

Ongoing adaptation: The application of machine learning methodologies allows for the continual retraining of models, enabling them to keep pace with the changing strategies of cybercriminals.

Facial age detection: This first stage involves the deployment of AI-enhanced facial recognition technology to estimate users' ages, which is then verified against the age

8 https://github.com/MahPascal/Figure-3.8-Three-Step-Model-for-Cybercrime-Identification/blob/main/README.md

they declared during the registration process. This mechanism is vital for maintaining compliance with age restrictions and for identifying accounts that warrant further investigation, especially in cases where minors may try to access harmful or inappropriate content. The facial recognition and age detection algorithms utilized are pretrained and are implemented in a secure manner that adheres to privacy compliance standards.

Content monitoring: The second step emphasizes the real-time examination of user-generated content to identify harmful or unlawful activities. Utilizing Natural Language Processing (NLP) models, text-based posts, messages, and comments are scrutinized to detect abusive language, threats, or illegal propositions. Additionally, computer vision models are employed to assess images and videos for explicit or illicit content. The content is systematically categorized according to themes such as violence, adult material, or fraudulent behavior, with unusual content-sharing patterns being flagged for further scrutiny. Sophisticated tools, including sentiment analysis and multi-label classification frameworks, facilitate accurate monitoring.

Cross-activities mapping: The final phase focuses on correlating user activities across multiple platforms to detect organized cybercrime. Behavioral trends, including shared IP addresses, device fingerprints, and usernames, are examined using graph-based analytics and big data tools. These analyses contribute to the mapping of fraudulent account networks, the identification of recurring violations, and the detection of suspicious interactions. By integrating multiple platforms and employing real-time activity mapping, organizations can swiftly respond to high-risk accounts, which may be flagged for suspension or referred to law enforcement for further action.

This systematic methodology integrates cutting-edge artificial intelligence technologies, multi-platform interoperability, and stringent privacy measures to establish an effective framework for detecting and mitigating cybercrimes across social media and the broader internet. Arora et al. [11] investigate the disparity between the requirements of online platforms for identifying harmful content and the trajectory of existing research initiatives. Their study underscores the difficulties associated with content moderation and offers perspectives on how research can better align with the needs of these platforms, proposing potential enhancements in the creation of effective tools for detecting harmful content in digital environments. Gongane et al. [31] investigate the present landscape of identifying and managing harmful content across social media platforms, highlighting both established methodologies and the challenges faced. The study provides a comprehensive review of different content moderation strategies and tools, assessing their efficacy in recognizing harmful material. Furthermore, it considers prospective advancements, particularly the integration of artificial intelligence, machine learning, and natural language processing to improve moderation frameworks, thereby fostering safer online spaces for users. In a study by Mah [60] focuses on enhancing cybersecurity through unbiased text categorization in IoT-based digital content using a Word-to-Graph model. This model transforms textual data into graph structures, enabling more accurate categorization and threat detection. By minimizing bias in data processing, it improves content filtering and security monitoring in IoT environments, ensuring robust protection against malicious content, cyberattacks, and unauthorized access in connected systems. Salminen et al. [81] present a study focused on the formulation of an online hate speech classifier applicable to numerous social media platforms. This research outlines a system that integrates machine learning and natural language processing techniques to facilitate the automatic detection and classification of hate speech across a variety of online contexts. The authors point out the challenges inherent in tailoring the classifier to different digital environments and emphasize its potential role in enhancing online safety and the effectiveness of content moderation strategies.

3.8 Conclusion

In summary, tackling challenges such as criminal activity, identity theft, misinformation, and the incitement of violence necessitates a comprehensive strategy that integrates strong identity verification mechanisms, technological advancements, and sound governance practices. The introduction of unique personal identity codes (ID Codes) presents a forward-thinking solution aimed at improving accountability and traceability across various platforms, including social media, dating applications, web browsers, and news organizations. By associating digital interactions with verified identities and utilizing AI-enhanced content moderation, both organizations and governmental bodies can substantially reduce risks while promoting safer and more transparent online spaces.

It is imperative for national authorities, technology companies, and global organizations to collaborate in order to create standardized measures that honor user privacy and mitigate malicious actions. These initiatives are not solely focused on fighting fraud or misinformation; rather, they aspire to reestablish trust in digital communications, enhance individual security, and preserve the integrity of online platforms, ultimately fostering a more resilient digital landscape on a global scale.

4 Internet of things psychological impact on knowledge acquisition based on natural language processing and virtual reality

Abstract: The swift advancement of the Internet of Things (IoT), Natural Language Processing (NLP), and Virtual Reality (VR) has profoundly altered the landscape of knowledge acquisition, human communication, cultural dynamics, cognitive states, and overall living conditions. Despite the progress facilitated by IoT, scholars continue to face significant hurdles in knowledge acquisition due to the absence of standardized methods, processes, and systematic organization for the storage and retrieval of digital information. This research introduces a scoring model, leveraging NLP techniques to evaluate and rank succinct, high-quality VR digital content. The model analyzes definitions of NLP sourced from four distinct databases: Science-Direct, University of York, IBM, and Wikipedia. The results indicate that while IoT enhances the global creation and dissemination of knowledge, it simultaneously contributes to content redundancy, complicating the retrieval of concise, high-quality information. The findings from a comparative analyses show variety scores, highlighting varying levels of internet content quality and the challenges associated with discerning the most reliable information. The study concludes that Social media and internet site offers succinct and high-quality variations in content, which influences users' psychological well-being through stress associated with information filtering.

4.1 Introduction

Internet queues and waiting lines on content is an important challenging part of human psychology that affect human beings. Modern developments of the internet of things (IoT) technology contributes to approximately 60 % of human social and emotional activities. The stress associated with sear queries often create a psychological negative impact on learner. Following advance and upraise in digitalization of education and business environment, internet access has become very important tool of technology application. Million needs has been slow down by information traffics, redundant data and similarity knowledge that comes with fatigue in determining right content. Virtual reality (VR) is the most widely used digital technology that connect humans with the external world through devices (Yin et al. [110]). Virtual reality can be regarded as the most achievable aspect of the term internet of things. This is because virtual reality technology connect living and non-living using gadgets and mounted head devices. Even though virtual reality has rightfully defined the term internet of things, but it has not succeeded in solving redundant data available across the globe that often create fatigue to online users.

https://doi.org/10.1515/9783112229750-004

Furtado et al. [30] said modern health management systems must have a queueing or waiting control system that can solves the psychological health impact network traffics creates on human psychology. Many studies indicates that network routers changes the path of network flow behavior over time and it affect human emotions. It is true because time factor affect the output of network. With adoption of IoTs that carry embedded sensor can always backup network changes when input data changes. The internet of things have capability to connect with objects. The capability of object sensors that operate on land surface where GPS signals are available can act always as balance-up for each needed input adjust.

Internet of Things (IoT) is a rapidly growing network that collect data, connect objects and exchange this data using embedded sensors with humans (Hasan and Al-Turjman [35], Khan et al. [45], Atzori et al. [13]). Internet based information traffic is becoming a common trend for online users. Internet capacity that enable the distribution of created data has a limited accessibility for remote activities due to data similarities. It's been observed during COVID-19 that most activities are moving remotely and there is need for scalability, elasticity and network security for all the created online datasets. Most embedded objects that connect with human using IoTs technology has a sense of artificial intelligence and cloud computing capabilities with IoTs sensors. Modern network security of deep supervised learning can work well on a selected network structure with hidden layers the chronologically arrange created datasets.

4.2 Literature review

This section is made up of definition of key terms, natural language processing and internet of things Psychological Impact, Supervised Learning Innovative Expectations on Virtual Reality, Natural Language Processing Content for Internet-based Data Extraction, Virtual Reality on User's Engagement, Types of virtual reality technologies that Swim across human physiology and Internet of things Elements that Impact Users Psychology,

4.2.1 Definition of key terms

Natural language processing (NLP). It is the deployment of computational approaches aim at and for the purpose of learning, understanding, and producing human language content (Zhou and Cheng [114]).

Virtual Reality (VR). The experience is designed as a simulation that leverages pose and portrayal actions through the tracking of 3D near-eye displays, which enhances the user's sense of immersion, imagination, engagement, and interactivity within a virtual realm (Aukstakalnis [14], Kekkonen et al. [44]).

Deep learning (DL). Deep learning represents a specialized approach within the broader field of machine learning, focusing on the acquisition of data representations

[52]. This method is characterized by its remarkable capacity and adaptability in learning processes. Furthermore, deep learning encompasses a body of knowledge that necessitates the separation of representation and learning, rather than relying solely on end-to-end learning strategies (Yan et al. [109]).

4.2.2 Natural language processing and internet of things psychological impact

Natural language processing (NLP) employs standard word processing techniques to manage text, treating it as a sequence of symbols while appropriately acknowledging the hierarchical nature of language. In the realm of natural language, multiple words form phrases, several phrases construct sentences, and ultimately, sentences express ideas. The implementation of NLP has significantly alleviated online stress for billions of users. Conversely, internet-based systems that lack NLP tools have adversely affected users' experiences. Users who struggle with online information without success may develop trauma, leading to various health issues. It is essential for industries, educational institutions, and knowledge development organizations to assess and enhance their systems to foster a user-friendly environment. A more complex website tends to create a more stressful experience for users. The detrimental effects of psychological stress on individuals are well recognized. Due to shifts in human behavior, software systems, administration, and various forms of documentation, certain information may not accurately represent the intended message. This study aims to facilitate the communication of information using the original data and text of the creator without altering its context, structure, or size. NLP presents a significant challenge in computer science, as human natural language is often imprecise and not straightforward (Ambriola and Gervasi [8], Way [106]). To comprehend human natural language, it is crucial to grasp not only the words but also the content, context, and underlying concepts. This understanding is vital, as the spoken content, concepts, and context reveal the creator's perspective and emotional state, which are unique to each individual.

Applications of natural language processing play a crucial role in ensuring secure communication and information management through the implementation of deep learning models, particularly in the context of digitalization within a virtual environment. Technologies such as digital twins, the Internet of Things, blockchain, big data, and cloud computing are transforming our conceptual frameworks (Kaur et al. [42]). Contemporary technological advancements are reshaping our understanding of the changes occurring in our surroundings, facilitated by innovative virtual reality tools. A significant challenge remains in enabling seamless data exchange to validate our health and enhance our well-being through virtual technologies, with security being a primary concern. While security threats are prevalent, there is a lack of a clear and comprehensive framework that addresses the broad spectrum of digital safety (Graff and Van Wyk [32]). This research presents a data security system known as the Scoring

Model. The Scoring Model is a structured approach designed to ensure secure communication between the sender and the intended recipient. This model offers multiple methods of securing communication through coding, allowing for information to be encoded using two-layer, three-layer, or additional methods, depending on the interaction between producers and users.

4.2.3 Supervised learning innovative expectations on virtual reality

Digital technologies play a crucial role in providing solutions to the challenges that arise from the economic and community transition to cloud systems. The implementation of deep supervised learning is an additional, powerful strategy in this regard (Manu [63]). Ensuring data security is essential for upholding human dignity and is a top priority for business development (Schmitt [84]). Machine learning has addressed a variety of issues, including data classification, prediction, forecasting, decision-making, and efforts to mitigate climate change. At present, security is a significant concern for the business sector, administrators, and IT professionals. This study outlines specific areas of concern for machine learning, which it designates as objectives necessary for effectively managing the security challenges that the world encounters.

The first objective is the need for a blended behavioral mindset change towards technological innovation. The effective management and collection of essential physiological data can significantly transform our perceptions, emotions, and mutual respect for privacy. This transformation necessitates the establishment of new regulations governing data usage and sharing. The recent advancements in digitalization have taken the world by surprise, highlighting the urgent need for education that equips individuals to comprehend and navigate their environments through virtual technologies. There is a pressing demand for a comprehensive technological framework that harmonizes with human existence and the current digital landscape. Machine learning exemplifies such technology, yet public training remains insufficient. Despite the availability of open resources, remote regions continue to lag due to inadequate internet connectivity, limiting their access to platforms like Jupiter, Anaconda, TensorFlow, and others. It is imperative that leading behavioral analysis software for human behavior research underscores the importance of universal access to knowledge and communication with specialists.

The second object is the need for a modernized socio-technical drivers that will accelerate a balance transitions. To effectively reduce the repercussions of data and security breaches, it is essential to initiate extensive transformations in the realms of electricity, internet access, limited privatization of network systems, and the establishment of autonomous technologies. The goal is to create a sustainable system that minimizes barriers, allowing individuals to access their needs without resorting to underground solutions. A shift towards a sustainable socio-technological mindset can be realized by directing efforts towards altering our perceptions of security issues, informed by an analysis of past reactions. The government must play a proactive role in combating security threats and cultivating a community-focused mentality. Security concerns should not be constrained by industrial regulations, cultural traditions, or political influences.

The last objective is the need for digital technologies that provide access to information, challenges, and impact on the globe. The global community must enhance its responsiveness to fragmented systems, limited data availability, and security breaches in order to establish a healthier and more equitable market environment, supported by intelligent automation. It is essential to optimize relationship management through the integration of intelligent servers, services, systems, and applications to effectively address the increasing demands of security. Digital factory solutions should collaborate closely with consultancy services and local stakeholders. This collaboration is vital, as both digital solutions and community consultancy serve as information and communication technology (ICT) tools that work together to better understand and address human needs and their implications. The disparity in access to ICT varies significantly worldwide, leading to substantial consequences. Numerous initiatives have been undertaken to bridge this digital divide, and if successful, they could facilitate a more coordinated approach to combat security breaches.

4.2.4 Natural language processing content for internet-based data extraction

This section provides natural language as a soft skill and hard skill. The features of natural language understanding deal with soft skills, human knowledge conveyed into text and speech while natural language generation deals with a hard skill which relates to

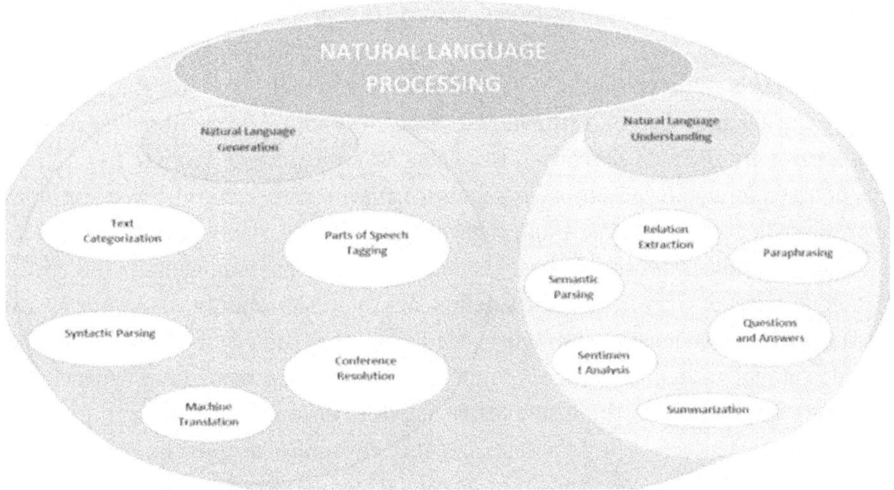

Figure 4.1: Natural language processing content for data extraction.
Source: Author's own work.

physical performance and structuring of the soft textual knowledge register as a text or spoken words that require manual arrangement.

Figure 4.1 illustrates the components of natural language processing and their interconnections with natural language. Natural Language Generation pertains to the activities of the writer or speaker (Liddy [56]). While primarily executed by computer scientists, the domain of natural language processing has garnered interest from linguists, psychologists, and philosophers alike (Lehnert and Ringle [53]). This highlights the significant impact of information technology. Through natural language processing, technology seeks to comprehend human emotions, responses, and perceptions via sentiment analysis. The rapid advancement of natural language processing has transformed it into a multidisciplinary field that bridges the gap between pure sciences and social sciences. Furthermore, natural language serves as a mechanism for applying learning techniques to automatically derive linguistic knowledge from natural language corpora (Brill and Mooney [19]).

4.2.5 Virtual reality on user's engagement

Human interaction with living and non-living entities, along with the pursuit of new skills, is profoundly shaped by the advancements in virtual reality technology. As noted by Wagler and Hanus [103], the engagement facilitated by virtual reality can exceed that of real-world interactions. This observation indicates that virtual reality may provide a clearer and more accurate representation of reality than what is perceived through human vision. Therefore, the process of content extraction is likely to be more efficient with virtual systems, as human observers may fail to capture certain information due to the inherent limitations of their eyesight. In contrast, virtual platforms reveal every detail, thereby promoting enhanced engagement. Pengnate et al. [75] investigate the role of presence in shaping user engagement and responses within 3D virtual reality settings, emphasizing its effect on perceived user value. The research delves into the connection between immersive experiences and user behavior, underscoring the significance of presence in augmenting value and engagement in virtual reality contexts.

Figure 4.2 illustrates the interactive components designed to facilitate the visualization of external cognitive artifacts, which are intended to assist users in their exploratory and sense-making endeavors. The factors that contribute to these activities include gaming, virtual exploration, communication, and participation in events. The outcomes associated with these supportive activities encompass enjoyment, personal growth, social connection, and the fostering of relationships between information and human responses. Data extraction must be conducted with an open mindset, devoid of emotional biases, which can be accomplished through comprehensive reinforcement training utilizing virtual technology to ensure that individuals remain unbiased.

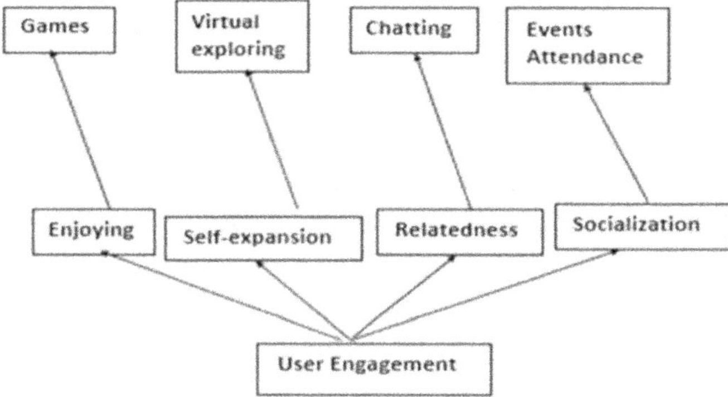

Figure 4.2: Virtual reality on user's engagement.
Source: Author's own work.

4.2.6 Types of virtual reality technologies that swim across human physiology

The ensuing paragraphs detail the services rendered by a digital system that elevates perception and insights into life. Through the use of virtual reality technologies, a meticulous engagement between humans and data is established (Flavián et al. [29]). This innovation allows individuals to foster a more precise orientation towards text classification and summarization, thereby meeting advanced extraction demands. Additionally, this technology not only offers comfort but also instills a greater yearning that real-life situations may lack.

Recreational real-world glasses. This approach employs a systematic methodology to enrich the imaginative experience prior to engagement. The advancement of virtual reality technology is propelling the development of innovative wearable glasses, which possess the capacity to enhance awareness of content before it is fully realized. This technological evolution is transforming our cognitive processes, emotional responses, and behaviors. Typically, the three-dimensional visualization of object identifiers through this technology diverges significantly from everyday experiences. Consequently, individuals utilizing recreational augmented reality glasses may respond differently to natural elements compared to their interactions with these elements in the physical world.

Simulation software systems. This technological framework emulates the functionality of a proposed system, offering empirical support for informed decision-making. Simulation software and applications are utilized to evaluate various scenarios or modifications in processes. A significant challenge within this framework is that actual outcomes from system trials often diverge due to the inherent variability of human behavior. Many users struggle to translate the skills learned through simulation software into practical applications in real-world situations.

Eye-tracking software systems. Eye tracking technology serves as a research instrument that observes, guides, regulates, and documents ocular behavior, including pupil movement and dilation in reaction to various stimuli. This eye-tracking software enhances the human capacity to concentrate on select items. However, users of this technology encounter significant challenges, which can lead to psychological complications.

Video Games. Video games represent sophisticated technological applications that offer numerous concealed advantages for individuals of all ages, ranging from cognitive stimulation to the enhancement of problem-solving abilities. Recent societal observations have noted a significant impact of gaming on attitudes, responses, communication styles, and interpersonal interactions.

3D printing. This technology operates systematically, employing computer-aided design to fabricate three-dimensional objects via a layering technique known as additive manufacturing. It is a rapidly evolving field that is increasingly influencing various sectors of contemporary society. The implications of 3D printing technology are reshaping environments, workplaces, educational institutions, and healthcare systems. The representations produced by 3D features often diverge significantly from real-world counterparts. This disparity between digital representations and physical reality profoundly impacts human perception.

Remote assistance. This feature allows users to view, control, and monitor a remote Windows computer over a network or the Internet, enabling the resolution of technical issues without the need for physical access to the machine. The visualization of virtual environments, classrooms, and open spaces is often consistent with visual perception when contrasted with both physical and virtual realities.

4.2.7 Internet of things elements of virtual reality that impact users psychology

In recent years, the convergence of technology has facilitated the integration of intelligent computing across a multitude of sectors. The advent of digital transformation, exemplified by the Internet of Things, has significantly impacted human psychological needs, largely attributable to the emergence of five digital platforms designed for the management of high-performance big data.

Sensors. The capabilities of internet sensors have brought considerable attention to the processes involved in locating, searching, identifying, and registering information. Today, businesses increasingly rely on Internet of Things (IoT) sensors to effectively navigate and identify prospective customers.

Collective-connectivity. The integration of non-living objects with living organisms is made possible through the connectivity provided by the Internet of Things. Presently, the IoT is adept at performing collective pairings of objects, thereby simplifying life for users.

Communication. The capability to communicate and share information through various platforms, including Microsoft Teams, Zoom, WebEx, WhatsApp, Instagram, and Facebook, is enabled by the advancements in the Internet of Things. The connection between people and devices, utilizing options such as audio, video, and chat features, would not be achievable without the evolution of IoT technologies.

Editing. Since the rise of internet tools, the conventional methods of writing and editing have experienced a remarkable shift. As a result, the processes of creating and modifying written content have become significantly easier than they were in earlier times.

Viewing. The capability to access, review, comment, and preview materials is greatly attributed to the development of internet services and applications. This advancement enables academics, editors, and students to manage and explore multiple datasets at the same time.

Rather et al. [79] analyze the engagement of tourists with brands that employ virtual reality, applying a uses-and-gratifications approach. This research highlights the impact of VR experiences on brand interaction, satisfaction, and loyalty, thereby contributing to the development of more effective tourism marketing strategies. The 4C framework, proposed by Rauschnabel et al. [80], seeks to offer an in-depth understanding of how consumers engage with augmented reality (AR). The study identifies four pivotal dimensions—content, context, consumer, and connection—that impact the level of engagement with AR technologies. This framework presents a comprehensive approach to enhancing AR experiences and strengthening consumer relationships.

4.3 Applied method

The methodological framework includes a series of defined steps. The investigation utilizes a scoring model, referred to as the scoring m-model data mining process, in conjunction with a behavior-oriented drive and influential function.

4.3.1 Scoring m-model steps for data process mining

This section outlines eight distinct steps necessary for constructing the data mining process associated with the scoring model. The steps are organized in chronological order, with each step serving a specific function and making a unique contribution to the overall data mining process.

Figure 4.3 illustrates the sequential steps employed in this study to classify the sample data. This procedure necessitates a straightforward yet rigorous approach that thoroughly examines the entirety of the textual data. The subsequent sections provide a detailed explanation of the data mining process.

Identification of data. The first step necessitates that the miner acquires an understanding of the dataset's display language. Upon identifying this language, the system analyst is able to advance to the process of data cleaning.

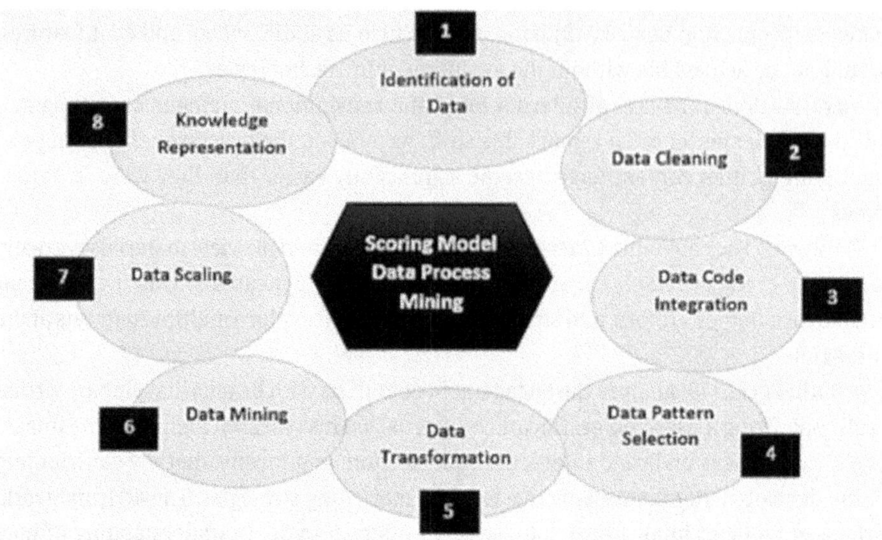

Figure 4.3: Scoring m-model steps for data process mining.
Source: Author's own work.

Data cleaning. In the second stage of data cleaning, it is essential for the data miner to expunge all punctuation symbols. Although the system does not permit the use of punctuation, the miner may choose to incorporate them. The exclusion of punctuation is justified by the requirements of data extraction and scaling processes.

Data code integration. The third phase pertains to the integration of data codes. During this stage, the miner is tasked with assigning numerical identifiers to each textual element discovered within the data corpus. This phase is of significant importance, as it lays the groundwork for the miner to assess the value of the data, whether through comparisons with other datasets or by evaluating the relevance of the content. It is imperative that this stage is approached with meticulous care, as any inaccuracies could result in erroneous data evaluations.

Data pattern selection. In the fourth step, the focus is on the selection of data patterns. This segment allows the miner to identify the requisite number of pattern layers for the process. The miner can handle all data through a two-line pattern, or alternatively, through a greater or lesser number of lines.

Data Transformation. The fifth step facilitates the alignment of textual data with the corresponding digital codes assigned to each element. This phase serves as the foundational stage for the construction of the pattern, taking into account the selection made in the fourth step. Within this section, the miner identifies each structure based on the chosen pattern from the previous stage.

Data mining. At the sixth step, the miner begins the fundamental extraction process, taking into account the morphologies of language. This research focuses primarily on the English language, with a significant emphasis on parts of speech. The metrics range and its alternatives are developed based on the structural components of parts of speech. The choice to employ parts of speech is predicated on their effectiveness in evaluating the relevance of speech and textual content.

Data Scaling. In the seventh step, the miner is equipped to evaluate and measure the dataset's value and relevance. Accurate data scaling hinges on the successful execution of the extraction process outlined in the sixth step. This extraction allows the miner to isolate meaningful content from that which is less significant. Once the extraction is properly conducted, the seventh step can achieve optimal performance in data scaling.

Knowledge representation. The eighth and final step permits the miner to showcase a dataset that features a clear scale, recognizable data patterns, and a data code indicative of the greatest relevance to unbiased content, in addition to the concentration of commonly used words (CFUW).

4.3.2 Behavior oriented drive and influential function

The data indicated in red in Figure 4.3 is classified as (content extracted), which constitutes the metric range substitute (MR^S). In contrast, the information presented in black, along with the elements highlighted in red, is categorized as (content extraction), forming the metric range (MR). To calculate the influence rate, the metric range substitute is divided by the total of the metric range and then multiplied by a behavior score of five (5). The behavior score symbolizes the five human sensory organs.

Definitions and formula

- D = Dependent parameters
- MR = Metrics Range
- MR^S = Metrics Range Substitute
- BS = Behavior Score or five sense organs
- KBS = Key Benefits Score

The equation for calculating E_q is defined as:

$$E_q = f(D) = \frac{\sum MR^S}{MR} \times BS \tag{4.1}$$

Example: push factors of e-services

- $MR = 36$
- $MR^S = 26$
- D = Dependent parameters

The above solutions provide the $f(D)$ values for each source based on the provided metrics range and substitutes.

The formula presented above explains the methodology for translating words into scores, which facilitates the evaluation of the relevance of each word in the context of the text.

4.4 Results

To achieve the results, the following methodological steps were implemented. Definitions were sourced from four separate webpages, a tool for parts of speech identification was selected, specific parts of speech were determined, a ranking list was compiled, and a scoring model graph was constructed.

4.4.1 Data

IBM: The branch of computer science and more specifically, the branch of artificial intelligence concerned with giving computers the ability to understand text and spoken words in much the same way human beings can.

Wikipedia: Is an interdisciplinary subfield of linguistics, computer science, and artificial intelligence concerned with the interactions between computers and human language, in particular how to program computers to process and analyze large amounts of natural language data.

University of York: Is a branch of artificial intelligence within computer science that focuses on helping computers to understand the way that humans write and speak.

Science-direct: Is a high throughput technology that enables generation of massive structured and codified data, applicable for clinical applications that promote efficiency in drug development and outcomes.

4.4.2 Parts of speech identifier

The following parts of speech were used to identify the metrics range substitutes and metrics range. The definition keywords identified as metrics range substitutes were considered very relevant to the knowledge require when considering natural language processing definition. (Nouns, adjectives, verbs, adverbs, interjections, prepositions, conjunctions, pronouns, determiners, and numerals.)

The ranking list was determined based on the part of speech identified using the parts of speech identifier. Each definition was encoded. The purposed of encoding part of speech identified in the definitions was to determined which definition is most relevant in content and not the volume of words used.

Table 4.1: Parts of speech analysis across sources.

Source	Nouns	Adjectives	Verbs	Other parts of speech
IBM	branch, computer, science, intelligence, ability, text, words, beings	artificial, spoken, human	understand	*Prepositions:* of, with, in *Conjunctions:* and *Determiners:* the, much, same
Wikipedia	subfield, linguistics, computer, science, intelligence, interactions, computers, data	interdisciplinary, artificial, natural, large	program, process, analyze	*Prepositions:* of, between, to *Conjunctions:* and *Determiners:* the, how, that
University of York	branch, intelligence, computer, science, computers, humans	artificial, human	focuses, helping, write, speak	*Prepositions:* of, within *Conjunctions:* that *Determiners:* the, way
Science-Direct	technology, generation, data, applications, efficiency, drug, development, outcomes	high, massive, structured, codified, clinical	enables, promote	*Prepositions:* of, for *Conjunctions:* and *Determiners:* the

Table 4.1 represents the selected parts of speech used in this study to demonstrate the application of (scoring m-model). From the ranking list, the words marked in red are identified as metrics range substitutes. The metrics range substitutes are those words that carry very high substance in the definition and contributes most to knowledge creation and understanding.

4.4.3 Statistical data

This section presents the statistical datasets derived from Figure 4.3. It offers a comprehensive breakdown of all definitions in accordance with the final scoring model.

- D = Dependent parameters
- MR = Metrics Range
- MR^S = Metrics Range Substitute
- BS = Behavior Score or five sense organs
- KBS = Key Benefits Score
- Equation:

$$Eq = \int (D) \frac{\sum MR^S}{MR} \times BS$$

Solutions

NLP definition by IBM

$$MR = 584, \quad MR^S = 479$$

$$f(D) = \frac{MR^S}{MR} \times BS = \frac{479}{584} \times 5 = 4.101$$

This section evaluate and score the definition of natural language processing based on information we extract from the IBM search engine

NLP definition by Wikipedia

$$MR = 666, \quad MR^S = 543$$

$$f(D) = \frac{MR^S}{MR} \times BS = \frac{543}{666} \times 5 = 4.076$$

This section evaluate and score the definition of natural language processing based on information we extract from the Wikipedia search engine

NLP definition by University of York

$$MR = 276, \quad MR^S = 235$$

$$f(D) = \frac{MR^S}{MR} \times BS = \frac{235}{276} \times 5 = 4.257$$

This section evaluate and score the definition of natural language processing based on information we extract from the University of York search engine

NLP definition by Science-Direct

$$MR = 351, \quad MR^S = 312$$

$$f(D) = \frac{MR^S}{MR} \times BS = \frac{312}{351} \times 5 = 4.444$$

This evaluate and score the definition of natural language processing based on information we extract from the Science-Direct search engine.

4.4.4 Scoring m-model content analyses of the definitions

The graph showcases the ranking of definitions in relation to their relevance. This part of the study focuses on the definition of natural language processing, employing the scoring m-model for analysis. The definitions reviewed include those from IBM, Wikipedia, the University of York, and the Science-Direct database, all evaluated with the scoring m-model.

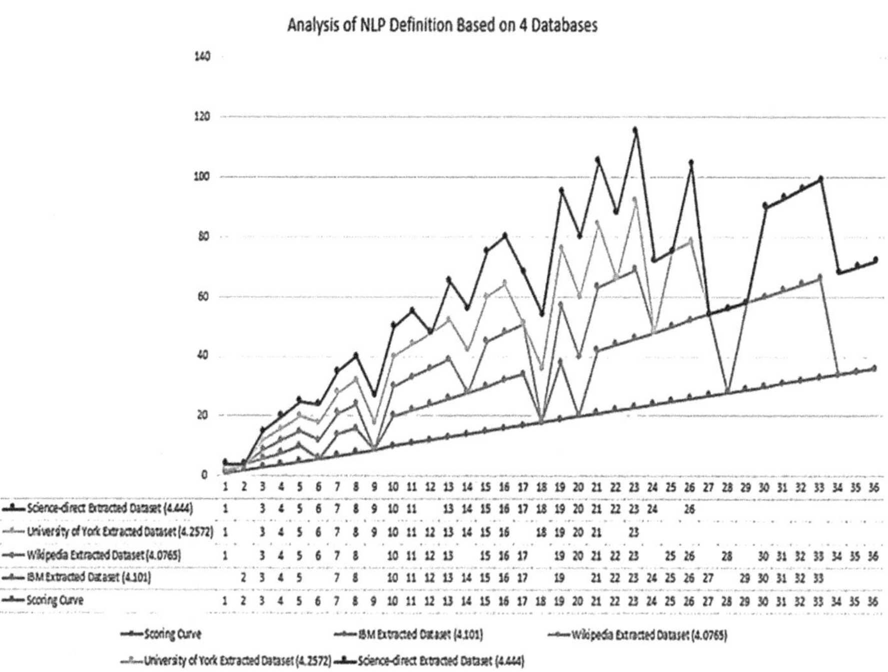

Figure 4.4: Scoring m-model content analyses.
Source: Author's own work.

Figure 4.4 illustrates the evaluation and ranking of definitions of natural language processing, focusing on the substance of the content rather than the quantity of words, their popularity, or the credibility of the hosting website. The analysis reveals that the most comprehensive definition is provided by ScienceDirect, achieving a score of 4.444 out of 5. Following closely is the University of York, which received a score of 4.257, while IBM's definition scored 4.1010. Wikipedia's entry, although informative, garnered the lowest score of 4.0765. This analysis underscores the importance of content quality over mere word frequency or popularity, indicating that the source of information is less significant in today's knowledge landscape. In the current digital age, particularly with the rise of the Internet of Things, the quality of information is paramount. The subsequent selection was made randomly to highlight the model's relevance and demonstrate how users can assess digital content. In the study by Mah [60], an unbiased approach to text categorization for IoT-driven digital content is explored through the implementation of a Word-to-Graph model. The research prioritizes the use of graph-based strategies to confront biases inherent in text classification within IoT frameworks. By organizing textual data into graph structures, the model seeks to enhance both the accuracy and fairness of categorization, thereby fostering a more nuanced understanding of context. The study illustrates its relevance in managing large volumes of IoT data while effectively minimizing bias, with experimental results validating its success.

4.5 Conclusion

The internet of things has created a virtual world and instill in it various aspect of life that take into consideration human social, economic, political, educational and emotional attributes with a strong bridge that connect knowledge acquisition and psychological needs. Numerous studies make us understand that the internet of things has soften the path and relationship between humans and objects. With the internet of things, it very easy to create knowledge, exhibit with virtual reality and share across the globe but at the same time makes it difficult to grasp concise quality knowledge within the created data due to a lot of content similarities. Every single user with access to the internet can generate as much content as possible. Creating knowledge without a proper storage achieve for potential users is absurd.

With the capability of internet of things, various technologies like virtual reality that used 3D technology to reinforce learning and knowledge creation has emerge. Virtual reality technologies of three dimensional technology (3D) which fully represent the term internet of things, have attempted to assist learners concentrate on a single item with the use of gadgets but have neither fully succeeded. Following these challenges associated with internet of things and virtual reality, the study proposed (scoring m-model) which is an NLP technique that can rank digital content and assist learners draw a knowledge scale of preference. The (scoring m-model) can assist learners achieve a positive psychological impact on knowledge acquisition, created content, and crowdsource multi-digital data.

General conclusion

Summary

The integration of Deep Learning (DL), Natural Language Processing (NLP), and advanced technologies such as IoT, RFID, and VR has significantly altered the dynamics of social media, particularly regarding the health, safety, and security of young individuals. This book provides a unified framework that addresses these critical challenges through innovative approaches.

Chapter 1 delves into the mechanisms of facial-age detection and content regulation, aimed at shielding teenagers from harmful online influences. Transitioning to Chapter 2, the discussion centers on AI-based security strategies that have shown effectiveness in preventing unauthorized access, fraudulent profiles, and breaches of privacy. Chapter 3 emphasizes the critical requirement for a global digital identification system to combat the increasing threats posed by cybercrime and the existence of untraceable online identities. In conclusion, Chapter 4 explores the capabilities of NLP-powered models to improve knowledge acquisition and evaluate content quality, addressing the challenges associated with the redundancy and unreliability of information available in digital formats.

This book promotes a transformative model for online engagement through the integration of various strategies that emphasize security, health, and digital ethics. The insights provided herein contribute to the establishment of a more secure, transparent, and inclusive digital landscape, thereby empowering users and encouraging responsible online conduct.

Future direction

Advancing deep learning and natural language processing methodologies for the immediate identification of harmful online content.

Examining Internet of Things (IoT) solutions for the proactive surveillance and mitigation of cyberbullying incidents in real-time.

Creating energy-efficient artificial intelligence architectures for the processing of extensive social media datasets.

Assessing the psychological effects of content moderation on the mental well-being of adolescents.

Broadening the scope of global digital identity frameworks to tackle issues related to privacy and ethical considerations.

Improving virtual reality technologies to foster educational and cognitive growth.

Utilizing blockchain innovations to enhance user authentication processes and safeguard data privacy.

Implementing longitudinal research to analyze the societal ramifications of AI-enhanced social media systems.

https://doi.org/10.1515/9783112229750-005

Bibliography

[1] Al Aziz R., Arman M. H., Karmaker C. L., Morshed S. M., Bari A. M., Islam A. R. M. T., Exploring the challenges to cope with ripple effects in the perishable food supply chain considering recent disruptions: implications for urban supply chain resilience, *Journal of Open Innovation: Technology, Market, and Complexity* **11** (1), 2025, 100449.

[2] Al-Sabti D. A., Singh A. V., Jha S., Impact of social media on society in a large and specific to teenagers, [In:] *2017 6th International Conference on Reliability, Infocom Technologies and Optimization (Trends and Future Directions) (ICRITO)*, IEEE, 2017, 663–667.

[3] Aldi M., Utilization of Tiktok application as Da'wah media and innovation in conveying Islamic values in the digital age, *LANCAH: Jurnal Inovasi Dan Tren* **3** (1), 2025, 32–41.

[4] Ali S., Youth, social media, and online safety: a holistic approach towards detecting and mitigating risks in online conversations, PhD thesis, 2024.

[5] Alim S., Cyberbullying in the world of teenagers and social media: a literature review, *International Journal of Cyber Behavior, Psychology and Learning (IJCBPL)* **6** (2), 2016, 68–95.

[6] Allen K. A., Ryan T., Gray D. L., McInerney D. M., Waters L., Social media use and social connectedness in adolescents: the positives and the potential pitfalls, *The Educational and Developmental Psychologist* **31** (1), 2014, 18–31.

[7] Alshamrani S., Studying users interactions and behavior in social media using natural language processing, 2021.

[8] Ambriola V., Gervasi V., Processing natural language requirements, [In:] *Proceedings 12th IEEE International Conference Automated Software Engineering*, IEEE, 1997, 36–45.

[9] Anderson I. A., Wood W., Habits and the electronic herd: the psychology behind social media's successes and failures, *Consumer Psychology Review* **4** (1), 2021, 83–99.

[10] Anwar N., Riadi I., Luthfi A., Forensic SIM card cloning using authentication algorithm, *International Journal of Electronics and Information Engineering* **4** (2), 2016, 71–81.

[11] Arora A., Nakov P., Hardalov M., Sarwar S. M., Nayak V., Dinkov Y., Zlatkova D., Dent K., Bhatawdekar A., Bouchard G., et al., Detecting harmful content on online platforms: what platforms need vs. where research efforts go, *ACM Computing Surveys* **56** (3), 2023, 1–17.

[12] Atallah R. R., Kamsin A., Ismail M. A., Abdelrahman S. A., Zerdoumi S., Face recognition and age estimation implications of changes in facial features: a critical review study, *IEEE Access* **6**, 2018, 28290–28304.

[13] Atzori L., Iera A., Morabito G., Understanding the Internet of Things: definition, potentials, and societal role of a fast evolving paradigm, *Ad Hoc Networks* **56**, 2017, 122–140.

[14] Aukstakalnis S., *Practical Augmented Reality: A Guide to the Technologies, Applications, and Human Factors for AR and VR*, Addison-Wesley, 2016.

[15] Barrett L., Ban facial recognition technologies for children-and for everyone else, *Boston University Journal of Science and Technology Law* **26**, 2020, 223.

[16] Behmann F., Wu K., *Collaborative Internet of Things (C-IoT): For Future Smart Connected Life and Business*, John Wiley & Sons, 2015.

[17] Biradar P., Kolsure P., Khodaskar S., Bhangale K. B., IoT based smart bracelet for women security, *International Journal for Research in Applied Science and Engineering Technology (IJRASET)* **8** (11), 2020, 688–691.

[18] Briandana R., Hesti S., Dwityas N. A., Social media and green consumption behaviour of generation Z, [In:] *Multi-Stakeholder Contribution in Asian Environmental Communication*, Routledge, 2025, 137–146.

[19] Brill E., Mooney R. J., An overview of empirical natural language processing, *AI Magazine* **18** (4), 1997, 13.

[20] Chen C., Entertainment social media based on deep learning and interactive experience application in English e-learning teaching system, *Entertainment Computing* **52**, 2025, 100846.

https://doi.org/10.1515/9783112229750-006

[21] Chhabra J. S., Chhajed A., Pandita S., Wagh S., GPS and IoT based soldier tracking & health indication system, *International Research Journal of Engineering and Technology (IRJET)* **4** (06), 2017, 1228–1232.

[22] Chua T. H. H., Chang L., Follow me and like my beautiful selfies: Singapore teenage girls' engagement in self-presentation and peer comparison on social media, *Computers in Human Behavior* **55**, 2016, 190–197.

[23] Collier H., Morton C., Teenagers: a social media threat vector, [In:] *International Conference on Cyber Warfare and Security*, vol. 19, 1, 2024, 55–61.

[24] Costa F., Genovesi S., Borgese M., Michel A., Dicandia F. A., Manara G., A review of RFID sensors, the new frontier of Internet of Things, *Sensors* **21** (9), 2021, 3138.

[25] Deep S., Zheng X., Jolfaei A., Yu D., Ostovari P., Kashif Bashir A., A survey of security and privacy issues in the Internet of Things from the layered context, *Transactions on Emerging Telecommunications Technologies* **33** (6), 2022, e3935.

[26] Dehshibi M. M., Bastanfard A., A new algorithm for age recognition from facial images, *Signal Processing* **90** (8), 2010, 2431–2444.

[27] Dennen V. P., Choi H., Word K., Social media, teenagers, and the school context: a scoping review of research in education and related fields, *Educational Technology Research and Development* **68** (4), 2020, 1635–1658.

[28] Dobák I., Thoughts on the evolution of national security in cyberspace, *Security and Defence Quarterly* 33 (1), 2021, 75–85.

[29] Flavián C., Ibáñez-Sánchez S., Orús C., Impacts of technological embodiment through virtual reality on potential guests' emotions and engagement, *Journal of Hospitality Marketing & Management* **30** (1), 2021, 1–20.

[30] Furtado D., Gygax A. F., Chan C. A., Bush A. I., Time to forge ahead: the Internet of Things for healthcare, *Digital Communications and Networks* **9** (1), 2023, 223–235.

[31] Gongane V. U., Munot M. V., Anuse A. D., Detection and moderation of detrimental content on social media platforms: current status and future directions, *Social Network Analysis and Mining* **12** (1), 2022, 129.

[32] Graff M., Van Wyk K. R., *Secure Coding: Principles and Practices*, O'Reilly Media, Inc., 2003.

[33] Gupta B. B., Quamara M., An overview of Internet of Things (IoT): architectural aspects, challenges, and protocols, *Concurrency and Computation: Practice and Experience* **32** (21), 2020, e4946.

[34] Hartwell G., Gill M., Zenone M., McKee M., Smartphones, social media, and teenage mental health, *BMJ* **385**, 2024, e079828.

[35] Hasan M. Z., Al-Turjman F., Optimizing multipath routing with guaranteed fault tolerance in Internet of Things, *IEEE Sensors Journal* **17** (19), 2017, 6463–6473.

[36] Hidayat R., Erniwati E., Ismail I., The impact of Facebook social media usage on the social relationships of teenagers in Makassar city, *Jurnal Ilmiah Mandala Education* **10** (1), 2024, 197–207.

[37] Huang G., Li D., Zhou S., Ng S. T., Wang W., Wang L., Public opinion on smart infrastructure in China: evidence from social media, *Utilities Policy* **93**, 2025, 101886.

[38] Jayaram K., Janani K., Jeyaguru R., Kumaresh R., Muralidharan N., Forest fire alerting system with GPS Co-ordinates using IoT, [In:] *2019 5th International Conference on Advanced Computing & Communication Systems (ICACCS)*, IEEE, 2019, 488–491.

[39] Jeong S. H., Kim H., Yum J. Y., Hwang Y., What type of content are smartphone users addicted to?: SNS vs. games, *Computers in Human Behavior* **54**, 2016, 10–17.

[40] Jia X., Feng Q., Fan T., Lei Q., RFID technology and its applications in Internet of Things (IoT), [In:] *2012 2nd International Conference on Consumer Electronics, Communications and Networks (CECNet)*, IEEE, 2012, 1282–1285.

[41] Jian T., Qi H., Chen R., Jiang J., Liang G., Luo X., Identification of tomato leaf diseases based on DGP-SNNet, *Crop Protection* **187**, 2025, 106975.

[42] Kaur M. J., Mishra V. P., Maheshwari P., The convergence of digital twin, IoT, and machine learning: transforming data into action, [In:] *Digital Twin Technologies and Smart Cities*, 2020, 3–17.

[43] Kaur S., Sumithran N., Rani M., Psychological factors behind status updates: a qualitative analysis of the display of personal information on social media, *BPA—Applied Psychology Bulletin (Bollettino di Psicologia Applicata)* **299**, 2024, 33–48.

[44] Kekkonen M., Frimponmaa Agyei E. E. Y., Meschtscherjakov A., Oinas-Kukkonen H., Personalized persuasive holograms: use case scenario-Running with arnold, [In:] *15th International Conference on Persuasive Technology, PERSUASIVE 2020*, RWTH Aachen University, 2020.

[45] Khan R., Khan S. U., Zaheer R., Khan S., Future Internet: the Internet of Things architecture, possible applications and key challenges, [In:] *2012 10th International Conference on Frontiers of Information Technology*, IEEE, 2012, 257–260.

[46] Khan S. I., Ray B. R., Karmakar N. C., Rfid localization in construction with iot and security integration, *Automation in Construction* **159**, 2024, 105249.

[47] Khoo B., RFID-from tracking to the Internet of Things: a review of developments, [In:] *2010 IEEE/ACM Int'l Conference on Green Computing and Communications & Int'l Conference on Cyber, Physical and Social Computing*, IEEE, 2010, 533–538.

[48] Kim Y., Sohn D., Choi S. M., Cultural difference in motivations for using social network sites: a comparative study of American and Korean college students, *Computers in Human Behavior* **27** (1), 2011, 365–372.

[49] Krishna D. H., Akshay S., Manikumar A., Sukumar D. H., Age Vision: AI powered facial age progression platform, *International Journal of Scientific Research & Engineering Trends* **10** (2), 2024, 286–291.

[50] Kuss D. J., Griffiths M. D., Online social networking and addiction—a review of the psychological literature, *International Journal of Environmental Research and Public Health* **8** (9), 2011, 3528–3552.

[51] Landaluce H., Arjona L., Perallos A., Falcone F., Angulo I., Muralter F., A review of IoT sensing applications and challenges using RFID and wireless sensor networks, *Sensors* **20** (9), 2020, 2495.

[52] Learning D, Deep Learning, High-Dimensional Fuzzy Clustering, Chicago: Chicago International Breast Course, 2020.

[53] Lehnert W. G., Ringle M. H. (Eds.), *Strategies for Natural Language Processing*, Psychology Press, 2014.

[54] Liang W., Xie S., Zhang D., Li X., Li K.-C., A mutual security authentication method for RFID-PUF circuit based on deep learning, *ACM Transactions on Internet Technology (TOIT)* **22** (2), 2021, 1–20.

[55] Lichy J., McLeay F., Burdfield C., Matthias O., Understanding pre-teen consumers social media engagement, *International Journal of Consumer Studies* **47** (1), 2023, 202–215.

[56] Liddy E. D., Natural language processing, 2001.

[57] Lin Z., Lin M., De Cola T., Wang J.-B., Zhu W.-P., Cheng J., Supporting IoT with rate-splitting multiple access in satellite and aerial-integrated networks, *IEEE Internet of Things Journal* **8** (14), 2021, 11123–11134.

[58] Liu H., De Costa M. F. S. D. C. B. M. F., Yasin M. A.-I. B., Ruan Q., A study on how social media influences on impulsive buying, *Expert Systems* **42** (1), 2025, e13448.

[59] Luthfi A. M., Karna N., Mayasari R., Google maps API implementation on IOT platform for tracking an object using GPS, [In:] *2019 IEEE Asia Pacific Conference on Wireless and Mobile (APWiMob)*, IEEE, 2019, 126–131.

[60] Mah P. M., Unbiased text categorization in IoT-based digital content using a word-to-graph model, *Procedia Computer Science* **251**, 2024, 31–40.

[61] Mah P. M., Skalna I., Offiong U. P., Virtual monitoring as a digital delivery and assessment impact on students' learning, 2022.

[62] Makarova E. A., Makarova E. L., Cyber-victimization and its impact on victim's psychosomatic status, *International Journal of Cognitive Research in Science, Engineering and Education: (IJCRSEE)* **11** (2), 2023, 231–245.

[63] Manu A., *Value Creation and the Internet of Things: How the Behavior Economy Will Shape the 4th Industrial Revolution*, Routledge, 2016.

[64] Marchi G., Mulloni V., Acerbi F., Donelli M., Lorenzelli L., Tailoring the performance of a Nafion 117 humidity chipless RFID sensor: the choice of the substrate, *Sensors* **23** (3), 2023, 1430.

[65] Mawaddah A. S. R., Ernawati R., Sureskiarti E., The influence of educational videos about factors influencing stunting through Twitter social media on the knowledge of teenagers at SMA Negeri 4 Samarinda, *Promotor* **7** (2), 2024, 299–303.

[66] McHugh B. C., Wisniewski P., Rosson M. B., Carroll J. M., When social media traumatizes teens: the roles of online risk exposure, coping, and post-traumatic stress, *Internet Research* **28** (5), 2018, 1169–1188.

[67] Montag C., Demetrovics Z., Elhai J. D., Grant D., Koning I., Rumpf H.-J., Spada M. M., Throuvala M., van den Eijnden R., Problematic social media use in childhood and adolescence, *Addictive Behaviors* **153**, 2024, 107980.

[68] Mudra G, Cui H, Johnstone M., Survey: an overview of lightweight RFID authentication protocols suitable for the maritime Internet of Things. *Electronics* **12**, 2023, 2990.

[69] Nikooghadam M., Shahriari H. R., Saeidi S. T., HAKECC: highly efficient authentication and key agreement scheme based on ECDH for RFID in IOT environment, *Journal of Information Security and Applications* **76**, 2023, 103523.

[70] Norval A., Prasopoulou E., Public faces? A critical exploration of the diffusion of face recognition technologies in online social networks, *New Media & Society* **19** (4), 2017, 637–654.

[71] O'Keeffe G. S., Clarke-Pearson K., et al., The impact of social media on children, adolescents, and families, *Pediatrics* **127** (4), 2011, 800–804.

[72] Orben A., Teenagers, screens and social media: a narrative review of reviews and key studies, *Social Psychiatry and Psychiatric Epidemiology* **55** (4), 2020, 407–414.

[73] Oshodi A., Enhancing online safety: the impact of social media violent content and violence among teens in Illinois, *World Journal of Advanced Research and Reviews* **23** (03), 2024, 826–833.

[74] Pachucki M. A., Breiger R. L., Cultural holes: beyond relationality in social networks and culture, *Annual Review of Sociology* **36** (1), 2010, 205–224.

[75] Pengnate S., Riggins F. J., Zhang L., Understanding users' engagement and responses in 3D virtual reality: the influence of presence on user value, *Interacting with Computers* **32** (2), 2020, 103–117.

[76] Ping H., Wang J., Ma Z., Du Y., Mini-review of application of IoT technology in monitoring agricultural products quality and safety, *International Journal of Agricultural and Biological Engineering* **11** (5), 2018, 35–45.

[77] Rahmatulloh A., Ramadhan G. M., Darmawan I., Widiyasono N., Pramesti D., Identification of Mirai Botnet in IoT environment through denial-of-service attacks for early warning system, *JOIV: International Journal on Informatics Visualization* **6** (3), 2022, 623–628.

[78] Rao P. M., Saraswathi P., Evolving cloud security technologies for social networks, [In:] *Security in IoT Social Networks*, Elsevier, 2021, 179–203.

[79] Rather R. A., Hollebeek L. D., Loureiro S. M. C., Khan I., Hasan R., Exploring tourists' virtual reality-based brand engagement: a uses-and-gratifications perspective, *Journal of Travel Research* **63** (3), 2024, 606–624.

[80] Rauschnabel P. A., Felix R., Heller J., Hinsch C., The 4C framework: towards a holistic understanding of consumer engagement with augmented reality, *Computers in Human Behavior* **154**, 2024, 108105.

[81] Salminen J., Hopf M., Chowdhury S. A., Jung S.-G., Almerekhi H., Jansen B. J., Developing an online hate classifier for multiple social media platforms, *Human-Centric Computing and Information Sciences* **10**, 2020, 1–34.

[82] Samee N. A., Khan U., Khan S., Jamjoom M. M., Sharif M., Kim D. H., Safeguarding online spaces: a powerful fusion of federated learning, word embeddings, and emotional features for cyberbullying detection, *IEEE Access* **11**, 2023, 124524–124541.

[83] Scanlon M., Digital forensics: leveraging deep learning techniques in facial images to assist cybercrime investigations, Felix Santiago, Anda Basabe, MSc, BEng, PhD thesis, University College Dublin, 2021.

[84] Schmitt M., Deep learning in business analytics: a clash of expectations and reality, *International Journal of Information Management Data Insights* **3** (1), 2023, 100146.

[85] Selnes F. N., Fake news on social media: understanding teens' (dis)engagement with news, *Media, Culture & Society* **46** (2), 2024, 376–392.

[86] Şen S. S., Cicioğlu M., Çalhan A., IoT-based GPS assisted surveillance system with inter-WBAN geographic routing for pandemic situations, *Journal of Biomedical Informatics* **116**, 2021, 103731.

[87] Shaik A., Bowen N., Bole J., Kunzi G., Bruce D., Abdelgawad A., Yelamarthi K., Smart car: an IoT based accident detection system, [In:] *2018 IEEE Global Conference on Internet of Things (GCIoT)*, IEEE, 2018, 1–5.

[88] Sheng M., Zhou D., Bai W., Liu J., Li J., 6G service coverage with mega satellite constellations, *China Communications* **19** (1), 2022, 64–76.

[89] Sheth A., Shalin V. L., Kursuncu U., Defining and detecting toxicity on social media: context and knowledge are key, *Neurocomputing* **490**, 2022, 312–318.

[90] Shokhrukh A., The impact of social media on teenage English slang: investigating the influence of platforms like Instagram and TikTok on the evolution of English slang among teenagers, Kokand University Research Base, 2024, 86–93.

[91] Smith T. R., No Time to cry over spilt milk: the effect of the European milk quota repeal on American dairy farmers, *Drake Journal of Agricultural Law* **21**, 2016, 217.

[92] Stewart K., Brodowsky G., Sciglimpaglia D., Two roads diverge in cyberspace: dual but opposing social media pathways affecting teens' well-being, *Young Consumers* **25** (2), 2024, 170–187.

[93] Stoyanova M., Nikoloudakis Y., Panagiotakis S., Pallis E., Markakis E. K., A survey on the Internet of Things (IoT) forensics: challenges, approaches, and open issues, *IEEE Communications Surveys & Tutorials* **22** (2), 2020, 1191–1221.

[94] Sun C., Application of RFID technology for logistics on Internet of Things, *AASRI Procedia* **1**, 2012, 106–111.

[95] Swan M., Sensor mania! The Internet of Things, wearable computing, objective metrics, and the quantified self 2.0, *Journal of Sensor and Actuator Networks* **1** (3), 2012, 217–253.

[96] Taneja P. P., Samsudin P. A. N., Honguan J. T., Sharsheeva A., Designing safe digital mental health and psycho-social support (MHPSS), 2023.

[97] Tartari E., Benefits and risks of children and adolescents using social media, *European Scientific Journal* **11** (13), 2015.

[98] Tatik T., Setiawan D., Does social media marketing important for MSMEs performance in Indonesia?, *Asia Pacific Journal of Marketing and Logistics* **37** (1), 2025, 99–114.

[99] Throuvala M. A., Griffiths M. D., Rennoldson M., Kuss D. J., A 'control model' of social media engagement in adolescence: a grounded theory analysis, *International Journal of Environmental Research and Public Health* **16** (23), 2019, 4696.

[100] Tsyhannyk O., The influence of social media on the development of children aged 13 to 15, 2022.

[101] Vannucci A., Simpson E. G., Gagnon S., Ohannessian C. M., Social media use and risky behaviors in adolescents: a meta-analysis, *Journal of Adolescence* **79**, 2020, 258–274.

[102] Veena K, Meena K, Kuppusamy R., Teekaraman Y., Angadi R. V., Thelkar A. R., Cybercrime: identification and prediction using machine learning techniques, *Computational Intelligence and Neuroscience* **2022** (1), 2022, 8237421.

[103] Wagler A., Hanus M. D., Comparing virtual reality tourism to real-life experience: effects of presence and engagement on attitude and enjoyment, *Communication Research Reports* **35** (5), 2018, 456–464.

[104] Wakchoure S. S., Shewale P. S., Rajput J. G., Gaupal S. A., Thakre M. P., Rade M. R., Multiple approach of RFID-based attendance system using IoT, [In:] *Soft Computing for Security Applications: Proceedings of ICSCS 2021*, Springer, 2022, 487–499.

[105] Wang S., Xu Q., Yi J., Multi-scale identification of driving forces for landscape ecological risk: a case study of the basin containing three plateau lakes in Yunnan, China, *Ecological Indicators* **170**, 2025, 113037.

[106] Way E. C., *Knowledge Representation and Metaphor*, vol. 7, Springer Science & Business Media, 1991.

[107] Wong D. S.-W., Fung S.-F., Development of the cybercrime rapid identification tool for adolescents, *International Journal of Environmental Research and Public Health* **17** (13), 2020, 4691.

[108] Yadav S., Kumari P., Sharma S., Kalra V., Sharma M., Batra B., Advanced molecular techniques in the identification of phytopathogenic fungi, [In:] *Molecular and Biotechnological Tools for Plant Disease Management*, Springer, 2025, 287–317.

[109] Yan L. C., Yoshua B., Geoffrey H., Deep learning, *Nature* **521** (7553), 2015, 436–444.

[110] Yin R., Wang D., Zhao S., Lou Z., Shen G., Wearable sensors-enabled human–machine interaction systems: from design to application, *Advanced Functional Materials* **31** (11), 2021, 2008936.

[111] Yu D., Zhou X., Noorian A., Hazratifard M., An AI-driven social media recommender system leveraging smartphone and IoT data, *The Journal of Supercomputing* **81** (1), 2025, 272.

[112] Zewude G. T., Natnael T., Woreta G. T., Bezie A. E., A multi-mediation analysis on the impact of social media and Internet addiction on university and high school students' mental health through social capital and mindfulness, *International Journal of Environmental Research and Public Health* **22** (1), 2025, 57.

[113] Zhang S., Liu M., Li Y., Chung J. E., Teens' social media engagement during the COVID-19 pandemic: a time series examination of posting and emotion on Reddit, *International Journal of Environmental Research and Public Health* **18** (19), 2021, 10079.

[114] Zhou Z., Cheng Q., Relationship between online social support and adolescents' mental health: a systematic review and meta-analysis, *Journal of Adolescence* **94** (3), 2022, 281–292.

Index

https://doi.org/10.1515/9783112229750-007

www.ingramcontent.com/pod-product-compliance
Lightning Source LLC
Chambersburg PA
CBHW081545220326
41598CB00036B/6570

* 9 7 8 3 1 1 2 2 2 9 7 4 3 *